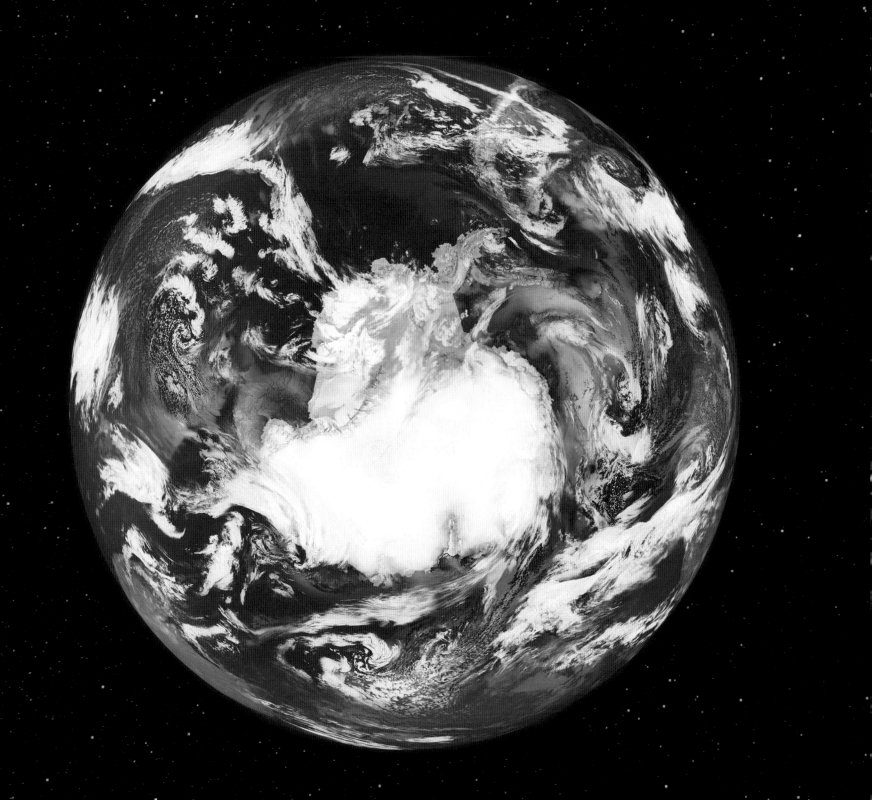

sally M. walker

Frozen Secrets
Antarctica Revealed

CAROLRHODA BOOKS • MINNEAPOLIS

For the many Earth scientists, past
and present, who have taught me
so much about our amazing planet.
—S.W.

Carolrhoda Books
A division of Lerner Publishing Group, Inc.
241 First Avenue North
Minneapolis, MN 55401 U.S.A.

Website address: www.lernerbooks.com

Library of Congress Cataloging-in-Publication Data

Walker, Sally M.
    Frozen secrets : Antarctica revealed / by Sally M. Walker.
        p.   cm.
    Includes bibliographical references and index.
    ISBN: 978–1–58013–607–5 (lib. bdg. : alk. paper)
    1. Antarctica—Juvenile literature. I. Title.
G863.W35 2010
919.8'9—dc22   2009034282

Manufactured in the United States of America
1 – DP – 7/15/10

The images in this book are used with the permission of: © NASA/Corbis Premium/
Alamy, p. 1; © Eastcott Mamoatiuk/Stone/Getty Images, p. 2; © Gordon Wiltsie/National
Geographic/Getty Images, p. 5; © Biosphoto/Dervaux Antoine/Peter Arnold, Inc., p. 6;
© Time & Life Pictures/Getty Images, p. 7; © INTERFOTO/Alamy, p. 8 (top); © The Image
Works, p. 8 (bottom); Scott Polar Research Institute, Cambridge UK/The Bridgeman Art
Library, p. 9 (top); © Jack Fletcher/National Geographic/Getty Images, p. 9 (bottom);
© Laura Westlund/Independent Picture Service, pp. 10, 13 (top) 29 (top), 38, 39 (left), 65,
71 (bottom), 72, 77 (bottom), 95; © Carlie Reum/National Science Foundation, p. 11 (top);
© Martin Harvey/Peter Arnold, Inc., p. 11 (bottom); © Buyenlarge/Time & Life Pictures/
Getty Images, p. 12; © Michael S. Nolan/Peter Arnold, Inc., p. 13 (bottom); © Central Press/
Stringer/Getty Images, p. 14 (all); © James Walker/National Science Foundation,
p. 15; © Josh Landis/National Science Foundation, pp. 16, 63; Douglas Wiens, Washington
University, St. Louis, MO, pp. 17, 35, 36; © Brien Barnett/National Science Foundation,
p. 18; © Michael Hixenbaugh/National Science Foundation, p. 19; © Classic Image/Alamy,
p. 20; © Reed Scherer, pp. 21 (left), 86 (all); © Galen Rowell/Mountain Light/Alamy, p. 21
(right); © Patrick Cullis/National Science Foundation, p. 22; © Cliff Leight/Aurora/Getty
Images, pp. 24, 48; © Kenneth Libbrecht/Visuals Unlimited, Inc., p. 25; Electron Microscopy
Laboratory, Agricultural Research Service, U. S. Department of Agriculture, p. 26 (all);
© Mike Embree/National Science Foundation, p. 27, 28; © David Vaughan/Photo
Researchers, Inc., p. 29 (bottom); © CNRS Photothèque, AUGUSTIN Laurent, p. 30;
© CNRS Photothèque/IPEV/FRENOT Yves, p. 31; © J.G. Paren/Photo Researchers, Inc.,
p. 32; © Peter Rejcek/National Science Foundation, p. 33; © Glenn Grant/National Science
Foundation, p. 39 (right); © Peter Johnson/CORBIS, p. 40; © Bryan & Cherry Alexander
Photography/Alamy, p. 41; © Corey Anthony/National Science Foundation, p. 42;
Ross Powell, p. 43, 44, 45; © Joseph Mastroianni/National Science Foundation, p. 46; Photos
courtesy of Stone Aerospace, pp. 47, 54, 55 (all), 56 (all), 57, 58, 59 (all); Photos courtesy of
Robin Ellwood, pp. 49, 50, 51, 60, 61 (all); © Liz Kauffmann/National Scienece Foundation,
p. 53; RADARSAT/GSFC/NASA, p. 64; © Science Source/Photo Researchers, Inc., p. 66;
© Andy M Smith/British Antarctic Survey/www.photo.antarctica.ac.uk, pp. 67, 97; © Neil
Ross/British Antarctic Survey/www.photo.antarctica.ac.uk, p. 68; © Christian Darkin/
Photo Researchers, Inc., p. 70; © Thomas Wiewandt/Visuals Unlimited, Inc., p. 71 (top);
William Hammer, pp. 73, 74 (all), 75, 76; © Franck Robichon/epa/Corbis, p. 77 (top); Allan
Ashworth, p. 79, 80 (all); Alexander Wolfe, University of Alberta, Edmonton, p. 81; Mark
Williams, University of Leicester, UK, p. 82; Peter Rejcec, Antarctic Sun, p. 83; NASA/
GSFC Scientific Visualization Studio, p. 84; © Pasquale Sorrentino/Photo Researchers,
Inc., p. 85; NASA images by Jeff Schmaltz, MODIS Rapid Response Team, Goddard Space
Flight Center, p. 87 (all); Michael Studinger, pp. 88, 93 (top); NASA, p. 89, 93 (bottom);
Lars Boehme, p. 90; CSIRO, p. 91; © Mark Brandon/British Antarctic Survey/www.photo.
antarctica.ac.uk, p. 92; © Kyle Hoppe/National Science Foundation, p. 94; © George
Steinmetz, p. 96; © Bettmann/CORBIS, p. 99. Backgrounds used throughout book:
© Arctic-Images/Iconica/Getty Images (ice); © Vassili Koretski/iStockphoto.com (ice crack).

Front cover: © Alex Taylor/British Antarctic Survey/www.photo.antarctica.ac.uk. Back
cover: © Vassili Koretski/iStockphoto.com (ice crack); © Arctic-Images/Iconica/Getty
Images (ice background).

Contents

PROLOGUE: MYSTERIOUS AND MAJESTIC 6

CHAPTER 1: GAINING A FOOTHOLD ON ANTARCTICA . . 11

Terra Australis Incognita 12

Taming the Frozen Frontier 14

Frozen Challenges .16

Happy Camper School 18

Who Does Science in Antarctica? 23

CHAPTER 2: ICE, ICE, AND MORE ICE 24

A Flake at a Time .25

The Ice Just Kept Spreading 28

Inside the Ice 30

Ice on the Move 33

Floating Ice 39

CHAPTER 3: BENEATH THE ICE 42

Mapping the World Beneath the Ice 42

Hitting Bedrock 43

Down in the Valleys 46

Water in the Dry Valleys 47

Dive! 49

A Robot Joins the Team 53

The Bot Goes Exploring 56

Still Waters Run Deep 62

CHAPTER 4: ONCE UPON A TIME 70

Fossils from the Journey South 70

Antarctic Dinosaurs 73

Freeze-Dried Surprises 79

CHAPTER 5: THE ANTARCTIC CRYSTAL BALL 84

Sifting through the Gaseous Clues 84

Thaw? 86

Antarctica and Earth's Oceans 89

Why? 95

AUTHOR'S NOTE 98

GLOSSARY 100

SOURCE NOTES 101

SELECTED BIBLIOGRAPHY 102

FURTHER READING AND WEBSITES 103

INDEX 104

Mysterious and Majestic

COLD IS PROBABLY THE FIRST WORD THAT COMES TO MIND WHEN YOU THINK OF ANTARCTICA. After all, *summertime* temperatures on the continent are often cold enough to make your teeth chatter. At their warmest, summer temperatures on Antarctica reach only 48°F (9°C). The bone-chilling winter temperatures on Antarctica make the freezer compartment of your refrigerator seem warm. Breathing is often done through a protective layer of cloth because sucking in a deep breath of frigid Antarctic air can make your lungs hurt. During the winter of 1983, Antarctica claimed the coldest temperature ever recorded on Earth: –128.6°F (–89.2°C).

Bleak. Forbidding. That's how most people think of Earth's remotest continent. Indeed, Antarctica's environment is so harsh that surviving more than a few days on the ice can be the stuff of movies. Film and television documentaries have captured the dramatic journeys penguins must make every year to survive on the ice. For humans, who are not as well suited for such an environment, the challenges are even greater. And yet, people have always risen to them. Humans seem to have known that Antarctica matters, despite its remote location at the bottom of the world.

Emperor penguins are one of the few species that can survive the winter on Antarctic ice.

In the early twentieth century, several groups set off to explore Antarctica. In 1910, the British explorer Robert Falcon Scott led one such expedition. Previous journeys on Antarctic ice had taught Scott to expect dangerous conditions, and he planned accordingly. Even so, less than a month into their new journey, blustery winds and violent seas plunged their ship on a treacherous roller-coaster ride. Supply crates burst loose on the deck. Pack ponies stumbled and fell. A sled dog washed overboard. Before they even set foot on Antarctica, the expedition members had received a harsh taste of Antarctic dangers.

Still, Scott and his men gamely set forth to explore Antarctica and claim its most coveted prize: being the first humans to set foot on the South Pole. Even harsher conditions on land eventually forced most of Scott's team to turn back. Scott and four others trekked on, though, convinced they could still be the first to the South Pole, despite dwindling supplies.

The competition to reach the South Pole was not his team's only focus. Along the way, Scott recorded all they saw and did in his journal, and the team collected many pounds of rocks and fossils.

Finally, in January 1912, they reached the South Pole, only to discover that another expedition, that of Roald Amundsen of Norway, had already been there and left thirty-five days earlier. Scott recorded his disappointment in his journal: "The Norwegians have forestalled us and are first to the Pole. It is a terrible disappointment, and I am very sorry for my loyal companions. . . . All the day dreams must go; it will be a wearisome return."

This was not the last cruel twist Antarctica had for Scott's team. With their precious supply of food and fuel quickly running

Members of Robert Falcon Scott's 1910–1913 expedition load a dog sled in sight of the ship *Terra Nova*.

out, the men trudged back toward the coast, their progress slowed by biting winds, deep snow, illness, and the heavy weight of their sleds. The team knew they had to cover a certain distance every day, and they knew that every day they were falling farther behind schedule. Tragedy struck first when team member Edgar Evans, stricken with frostbite and fatigue, collapsed and died one month into the return trip. A month later, Lawrence Oates, hobbled by severely frostbitten feet, decided that his companions stood a better chance without him slowing them down. Scott wrote in his journal that one night Oates told the others "I am just going outside and may be some time." Then he stepped out of the tent into the storm, knowing he would certainly die. His sacrifice was not enough, though. The remaining members of the team continued for another nine days before fatigue, frostbite, hunger, and blizzard conditions overcame them. They all died together around March 29, 1912, only 11 miles (18 kilometers) from the supply depot, where food and fuel awaited.

Top: Men and dogs worked side by side pulling sleds loaded with supplies as well as specimens. *Above:* Members of the Terra Nova Expedition at the South Pole. Standing from left to right, Lawrence Oates, Scott, and Edgar Evans; seated, Henry Bowers and Edward Wilson.

Scott, a scientist to his last breath, continued to write in his journal and to write letters to friends and family to the very end. In a letter, he implored his wife to make their young son "interested in natural history." The following season, when other members of the expedition reached Scott's last camp, they recovered the journals, letters, and the photographs and specimens the team had collected. Though Scott and his companions had perished, the precious few secrets of Antarctica they'd uncovered survived.

Without question, Antarctica is a land of endless cold and merciless challenges to survival. But the final impression you get from Antarctica, the last word on the continent, is *mysterious*. Antarctica guards its secrets closely, and somehow, that makes them all the more worth finding and all the more important. Conditions on Antarctica are still cruel today. The glory of being first to the South Pole or first to cross the continent has been claimed. And yet men and women are still drawn to study Antarctica. They know, as even those early explorers knew, that the continent is a place of great importance to our future understanding of Earth. The scientists who work on Antarctica follow in Scott's footsteps and even live near the preserved ruins of his camp. They study Antarctica's ice and rock and its water, plants, and animals. They look into its past in hopes of better understanding its future and maybe the future of Earth and its inhabitants. And as they do, they must brave Antarctica's hardships and confront its mysteries if they hope to reveal its frozen secrets.

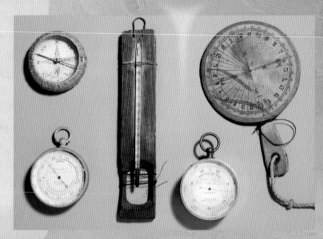

Below: Clockwise from upper left, Robert Falcon Scott's compass, thermometer, sundial, altitude scale, and barometric scale from the Terra Nova Expedition. *Bottom:* Rocky mountaintops poke through the ice near the South Pole.

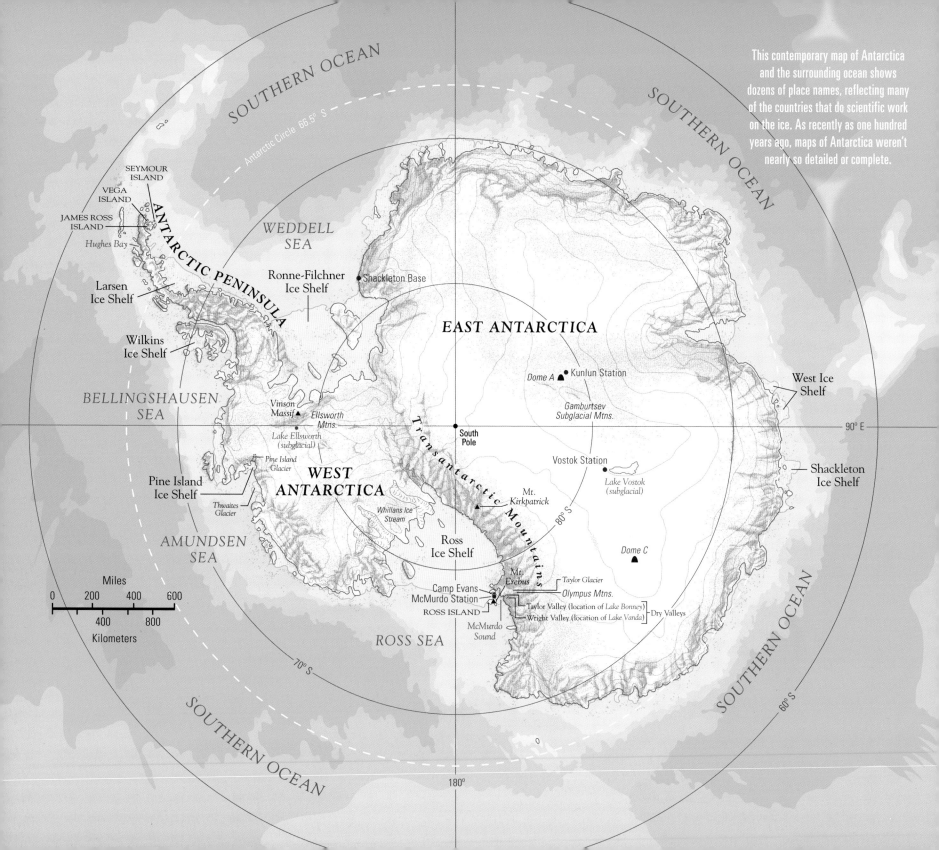

SOUTHERN OCEAN

SOUTHERN OCEAN

SOUTHERN OCEAN

SOUTHERN OCEAN

This contemporary map of Antarctica and the surrounding ocean shows dozens of place names, reflecting many of the countries that do scientific work on the ice. As recently as one hundred years ago, maps of Antarctica weren't nearly so detailed or complete.

Antarctic Circle 66.5° S

SEYMOUR ISLAND

VEGA ISLAND

JAMES ROSS ISLAND

Hughes Bay

ANTARCTIC PENINSULA

WEDDELL SEA

Larsen Ice Shelf

Ronne-Filchner Ice Shelf

Shackleton Base

EAST ANTARCTICA

Wilkins Ice Shelf

Dome A • Kunlun Station

BELLINGSHAUSEN SEA

West Ice Shelf

Vinson Massif ▲ Ellsworth Mtns.

Gamburtsev Subglacial Mtns.

90° E

Lake Ellsworth (subglacial)

South Pole

Pine Island Glacier

Vostok Station

Pine Island Ice Shelf

WEST ANTARCTICA

Shackleton Ice Shelf

Lake Vostok (subglacial)

Thwaites Glacier

Whillans Ice Stream

Mt. Kirkpatrick ▲

80° S

AMUNDSEN SEA

Ross Ice Shelf

Dome C ▲

Mt. Erebus

Taylor Glacier

Miles

Camp Evans
McMurdo Station

Olympus Mtns.

0   200   400   600

ROSS ISLAND

Taylor Valley (location of Lake Bonney)

Dry Valleys

400   800

McMurdo Sound

Wright Valley (location of Lake Vanda)

Kilometers

ROSS SEA

70° S

60° S

SOUTHERN OCEAN

180°

CHAPTER 1

Gaining a Foothold on Antarctica

ALMOST ONE HUNDRED YEARS AFTER SCOTT, A SCIENTIFIC RESEARCH TRIP TO ANTARCTICA IS STILL A SERIOUS UNDERTAKING, EVEN WITH MODERN TRANSPORTATION AND TECHNOLOGY. Scientist William Hammer's regular laboratory is at Augustana College in Rock Island, Illinois, where the average summer temperature is 76°F (24°C), but he also does research 10,000 miles (16,000 km) away in the interior of Antarctica, where the average summertime temperature is –20°F (–29°C). To get there, he and his team take a thirty-hour flight from the United States to New Zealand, where they pick up cold-weather gear. Then, in an LC-130 cargo plane, they fly to McMurdo Station on Ross Island, another eight- to ten-hour flight. LC-130s are equipped with wheels for landing on normal paved runways, but they also have ski-equipped landing gear for touchdowns on snow and ice, the materials that "pave" Antarctic runways.

At McMurdo, they stock up with the food and equipment they need to survive while working in the field, or away from research stations, for periods lasting from three to ten weeks. "During that time we don't plan on receiving new supplies regularly. We pretty much take everything we need for the season with us," Hammer explained. Finally, Hammer's crew takes off in another ski-equipped airplane that leaves them on the flanks of Mount Kirkpatrick in the Transantarctic Mountains range, where they set up their base camp.

Tourists who visit Antarctica may have more comfortable shipboard living quarters than scientists working in the field, but tourists still must follow certain rules and they're still subject to

Above: A U.S. Air Force LC-130 cargo plane lands at McMurdo Station, a research center operated by the United States, on Ross Island. The craft is equipped with skis for landing gear. *Left:* Tourists come ashore on Antarctica in inflatable boats—if weather permits.

the continent's weather. More than thirty thousand tourists visit Antarctica on ships each year. Protecting the Antarctic environment from damage is crucial, so all activities must be planned with this in mind. To minimize the environmental impact of tourism, small groups of tourists from these ships take turns visiting the mainland via small inflatable boats. But the sea surrounding Antarctica is no less unpredictable than it was two centuries earlier. At the first signs of furious water, all trips to the mainland via the inflatable craft are canceled.

TERRA AUSTRALIS INCOGNITA

While it may not be an easy journey, at least modern visitors know where Antarctica is. This hasn't always been the case. Antarctica's first frozen secret was its location. As far back as ancient Greece, geographers had believed that a continent existed, in Earth's southernmost reaches. One of them, a Roman citizen named Ptolemy, even gave the undiscovered continent a name, calling it Terra Australis Incognita. In Latin, this means "unknown southern land." But not until the 1700s were explorers and sailors able to brave uncharted seas in hopes of a glimpse of the mysterious land.

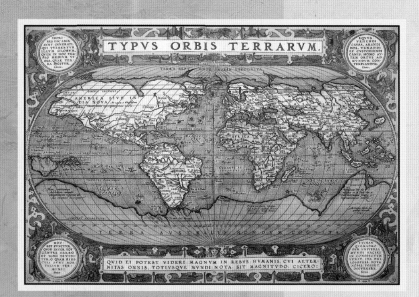

A map of Earth created in the 1700s showing Terra Australis Nondum Cognita—meaning "southern land not yet known"—in the place of Antarctica. Humans would not set foot on Antarctica until over two centuries later.

The British explorer Captain James Cook made history on January 17, 1773, when his ship *Resolution* sailed into an area called the Antarctic Circle—the first ship to do so. How did he know he did it? Because he kept track of the *Resolution*'s position on Earth's surface with a map and an instrument called a sextant. A sextant measures the angle between the sun's position in the sky and the horizon. Cook used the angle to determine *Resolution*'s latitude on a map. Cook's sextant eventually showed him they'd crossed the latitude line labeled 66.5 degrees south. His was the first ship to do so. He and his crew were confident that they would soon see the undiscovered continent!

But Antarctica's challenges proved too perilous for *Resolution*. With curtains of water sheeting from their edges, icebergs—gigantic chunks and slabs of floating ice—rise and fall

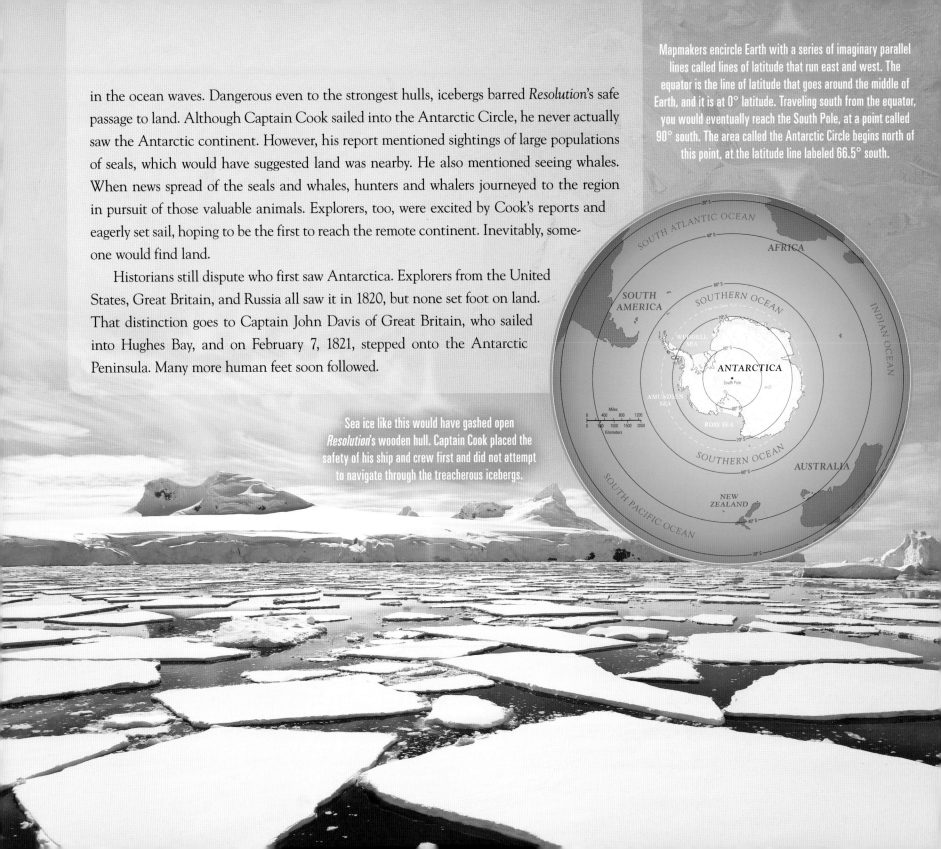

in the ocean waves. Dangerous even to the strongest hulls, icebergs barred *Resolution*'s safe passage to land. Although Captain Cook sailed into the Antarctic Circle, he never actually saw the Antarctic continent. However, his report mentioned sightings of large populations of seals, which would have suggested land was nearby. He also mentioned seeing whales. When news spread of the seals and whales, hunters and whalers journeyed to the region in pursuit of those valuable animals. Explorers, too, were excited by Cook's reports and eagerly set sail, hoping to be the first to reach the remote continent. Inevitably, some-one would find land.

Historians still dispute who first saw Antarctica. Explorers from the United States, Great Britain, and Russia all saw it in 1820, but none set foot on land. That distinction goes to Captain John Davis of Great Britain, who sailed into Hughes Bay, and on February 7, 1821, stepped onto the Antarctic Peninsula. Many more human feet soon followed.

Mapmakers encircle Earth with a series of imaginary parallel lines called lines of latitude that run east and west. The equator is the line of latitude that goes around the middle of Earth, and it is at 0° latitude. Traveling south from the equator, you would eventually reach the South Pole, at a point called 90° south. The area called the Antarctic Circle begins north of this point, at the latitude line labeled 66.5° south.

Sea ice like this would have gashed open *Resolution*'s wooden hull. Captain Cook placed the safety of his ship and crew first and did not attempt to navigate through the treacherous icebergs.

Vivian Fuchs (inset and standing next to Sno-Cat) led the first team to cross Antarctica. Almost fifty years after Scott, Fuchs's expedition relied on Sno-Cats and supplies dropped from airplanes.

TAMING THE FROZEN FRONTIER

By the 1950s, humans had mastered Antarctica's challenges well enough to spend long periods of time on the ice. As a result, more of Antarctica's secrets began to be revealed, but not without considerable efforts, both physical and diplomatic.

An international community of scientists designated the period of time from July 1, 1957, to December 31, 1958, as the International Geophysical Year (IGY). During this time, researchers from twelve countries flocked to Antarctica, establishing more than fifty stations from which they could collect scientific data about the continent.

One of the accomplishments of the IGY was the first transcontinental crossing of Antarctica. That journey began in November 1957, when explorer Vivian Fuchs and his twelve-man team set out in a convoy from Shackleton Base, located on the Weddell Sea. Their expedition, along with equipment provided by five nations, rode in tractors that were specially adapted for traveling across icy terrain and in Sno-Cats, vehicles with conveyor-belt-like treads for traveling on snow. Fuchs's expedition crossed the South Pole on January 19, 1958, and then continued on to complete their trip at Scott Base on Ross Island on March 2, 1958. The entire journey was 2,158 miles (3,473 km). Unlike Amundsen's or Scott's expeditions to the South Pole, the transcontinental team was assisted by supply airplanes that deposited equipment and also provided the team with reconnaissance of the terrain. With an enormous collaborative effort, humans had finally crossed the surface of Antarctica more than 120 years after they had first landed on the continent.

The international community has recognized the unique place Antarctica holds as one of Earth's last largely unexplored and unpopulated frontiers. The continent has no permanent residents and no native peoples. To manage such a place required unique cooperation among many nations. All twelve of the IGY countries agreed that the exploration of this continent is the right of Earth's people and that the knowledge obtained should be shared. In support of this belief, the twelve nations signed an agreement called the Antarctic

Treaty, which went into effect in 1961. Among other things, the treaty stipulates that Antarctica shall be used for peaceful purposes only. No wars can be fought there, and militaries can only be used to bring in researchers and supplies necessary for scientific research or for other peaceful purposes. The scientists from all countries must freely share the information they obtain. The continent cannot be exploited for any natural resources that it might contain, including fossil fuels like oil and coal. Any nuclear explosions are prohibited, as is the disposal of radioactive waste. As of 2008, forty-seven countries had signed the agreement.

McMurdo Station during Antarctica's five months of winter darkness. Only a handful of people remain at the station between April and August, when temperatures plummet and the sun never rises.

Tiny rock particles blown by powerful Antarctic winds wear away boulders and cliffs like superstrong sandpaper. Sometimes wind-carved rock takes on interesting forms, like the elephant-shaped ventifact in the Wright Valley.

Since the Antarctic Treaty went into effect, additional agreements have extended its scope to protect the continent's environment, its animals and plants, the historic buildings and sites from early explorers, and the management of tourism. Tourist access to the shore is also limited by the treaties and rules that govern those who visit because any person who sets foot on Antarctica could change its environment. Controlling access to the continent protects Antarctica's environment from damage.

Antarctica continues to maintain its claim as Earth's most remote and forbidding continent. However, in the last century, people have established not only a physical presence on the continent but have also managed to come to a consensus on how scientific research will proceed.

FROZEN CHALLENGES

Although Antarctica has no permanent residents, during the summer as many as a few thousand scientists conduct research on the continent. While they're in the field, they can face challenges and dangers that range from wind to fire to—of course—ice.

The katabatic winds, which form when cold air rolls down from a mountain toward lower-lying coastal areas, can gust over 200 miles (322 km) per hour—among the highest winds ever recorded on Earth. Antarctica veteran Robin Ellwood is always amazed by the ever-changing Antarctic winds.

"It can be everything from a gentle whooshing breeze to a hurricane-force blow-down! When you're near a large, intricate ventifact—a rock sculpted by wind—the wind passing around the various angles makes a melodious sound. Sometimes it almost sounds like harps! Other times, when the wind is stronger, it sounds as if the valley where we are working is growling. I have been in winds that just about knock you over!" Ellwood explained.

Air can be an obstacle even when the wind isn't blowing. Those who will be working in Antarctica's mountainous regions learn how to hike and climb at altitudes where the air is thin—that is, where there are significantly fewer oxygen molecules per square foot than there are at sea level. The simple act of breathing becomes a challenge in this rarefied air. Headaches, fatigue, nausea, and other symptoms of altitude sickness plague those who don't take precautions and learn to breathe properly in these areas.

And some people do seek Antarctica's high points. Located in the Ellsworth Mountains, 750 miles (1,200 km) from the South Pole, the Vinson Massif towers skyward. At 16,050 feet (4,892 meters), the Vinson Massif is the continent's highest mountain. As such, it is one of Earth's Seven Summits, the highest mountains on each of Earth's seven continents. Any mountain climber who seeks to join the ranks of the Seven Summits group of elite climbers must reach the top of the Vinson Massif. Peter Athans is one member of this club. Athans has summited Mount Everest seven times and is one of the best mountain climbers in the world, but in all of his travels, Antarctica is in a separate category. "In the Himalaya, the region in Asia where Mount Everest is located, one travels through a variety of environmental and cultural zones before getting close to the glaciers; not so with the Antarctic. From the beginning, one lands on an ice sheet, the expedition takes place and then one leaves from the same place. Frequently, it feels like being on another planet."

Making a shelter in the wind is just one of the challenges scientists face in Antarctica. Geologist Douglas Wiens and colleagues struggle to set up a Scott tent.

In such an extremely cold environment, one might not immediately think of fire as an Antarctic hazard. But fire is one of two "burns" that geologist Ross Powell always keeps in mind when working in Antarctica. "Fire at a base camp is bad—the British had one just a few years ago. And fire can occur at a field camp, where you are cooking in a tent." The loss of shelter due to fire could have tragic consequences.

The second kind of "burn" that Powell worries about is frostbite. "Frostbite tops the list. People still get frostbite even with all of the modern clothing. It's especially true if you are working outside and sweat and then have no warm structure to dry everything out properly."

In severe frostbite cases, the skin turns a whitish purple color, and the damage to tissue may be so great that the person will lose fingers, toes, or the tips of the nose and the ears. The proverb "better safe than sorry" definitely holds true in Antarctica.

On the other hand, sometimes ice isn't quite frozen solid enough. Powell recalled one potentially hazardous situation that occurred when he was working on a sediment drilling project in the Ross Sea, near Cape Roberts. "We were working pretty close to the ice edge on thick ice that overlies the ocean and a big storm came through. It blew a huge amount of sea ice out and we ended up being about half a mile [1 km] from the ice edge. That was considered too dangerous, so drilling had to be abandoned for the season. We've also had to postpone seasons because the sea ice didn't form thick enough to support the weight of the drill rig." Without a doubt, Antarctica presents scientists with challenges unlike any other research site on Earth.

HAPPY CAMPER SCHOOL

What do scientists need to survive all this? First off, anyone who plans on spending any amount of time outdoors must dress warmly—especially those who are working in the field far from research stations. Antarctica is one of the few places where what you put on in the morning to go to work is a life-or-death decision. In Scott and Amundsen's time, explorers suited up with layers of woolen clothing; jackets; boots; and large, furry, animal-skin mittens. A woolen hoodlike garment called a balaclava covered the head, the neck, and the ears and kept out drafts along the collar of the jacket. The problem was, these materials didn't take into account one important fact: hot people sweat. Even in frigid temperatures, people who are expending energy generate heat and can still work up a sweat. If clothing can't "breathe," allowing sweat to escape, a person's clothes get damp. As the person cools down after activity stops, wet clothing makes the person even colder. Modern scientists still wear layers of clothing; they're just made of new kinds of materials, such as polypropylene fleece. And most of the garments are no different from those that people who live in cold climates regularly wear for outdoor activities. Outerwear starts with a hooded parka

Serious cold calls for serious boots. These boots—sometimes called Mickey Mouse, or bunny, boots—were developed for the U.S. Army.

and a pair of lightweight wind pants that ward off blasting Antarctic wind gusts. Two pairs of pants are worn beneath the wind pants for insulation. And beneath those pants is a set of long underwear made of synthetic fabrics woven in a way that draws sweat away from the body. Boots are made to hold layers of air that act as insulation for the foot. Gloves, sometimes worn more than one pair at a time, complete the outfit. Although Antarctica is not like a typical day at the beach, sunscreen and goggles (or sunglasses) complete the "outfit" for everyone who will be outside for all but a few minutes. Sunburn and snow blindness are real and present dangers.

Outfitting themselves with warm clothes is just the first step in getting prepared for fieldwork. Before leaving main scientific research stations like the U.S. McMurdo Station, scientists must also attend survival school, which pupils refer to as Happy Camper School. For about two weeks, members of the McMurdo Station search-and-rescue staff teach scientists and anyone else new to Antarctica survival skills. Among other things, students learn how to recognize and cross crevasses—the deep cracks that riddle glacial surfaces. They learn how to hike and climb under stressful conditions. They learn how to tie knots in safety ropes, to climb ice-covered rock cliffs, and to identify dangerous areas. They are taught how to pack snow to form a shelter, and then they're asked to spend a night inside it. Cold air can't seep through the shelter's tightly packed snow walls and ceiling, and the body heat and breath of the occupants gradually heats up the air inside. A solidly built snow shelter is almost like a cocoon, keeping its residents snug and warm. Students in Happy Camper School, especially those who venture out into remote field camps, must learn some find-and-rescue strategies as well.

Happy Camper School students build a snow shelter called a *quinzee*. In an emergency, a scientist in the field could stay warm overnight in such a shelter.

Planning for Survival

The vast majority of scientists on Antarctica won't have to call on the survival *and* rescue skills they learn in Happy Camper School. But planning for the worst has a long history in Antarctic exploration. Roald Amundsen wrote in his autobiography that planning and preparedness were the reasons he reached the South Pole first and returned safely. "I may say that this is the greatest factor—the way in which the expedition is equipped—the way in which every difficulty is foreseen, and precautions taken for meeting or avoiding it. Victory awaits him who has everything in order—luck, people call it. Defeat is certain for him who has neglected to take the necessary precautions in time; this is called bad luck."

Norwegian explorer Roald Amundsen poses at the South Pole with his sled dogs. Amundsen's expedition was the first to reach the South Pole, beating Scott's Terra Nova team by a month.

Robin Ellwood recalled one of her Happy Camper School exercises. Successful completion required setting up a way to stay connected with one another, while leaving the safety of the tent.

My instructors invented a missing team member crisis—someone had gone to the outhouse and not returned. Our task was to find him/her. In order to simulate "white out" conditions that could occur in serious weather conditions, we had to place big white buckets over our heads. This left us unable to see and unable to hear very well, just as it would be under windy conditions. We really had to yell in order for others to hear us. It was quite an amusing sight to see everyone stumbling around out on the ice sheet with white buckets on our heads—especially since the buckets all had faces drawn on them. The lesson was effective though! We learned how to set up a rope system that allowed us to stay connected to the main camp, but also to set up a search pattern for the missing person. We did eventually find the person (who was beside the outhouse)!

Antarctica is intolerant of foolhardy behavior, so scientists take learning these survival skills seriously. Mastering these skills can easily be the difference between life and death.

Once in the field, the skills learned at Happy Camper School are combined with certain in-camp rules that further ensure everyone's safety. Rules such as never traveling alone, keeping your radio warm (so it works), and bringing an emergency survival pack with you at all times are standard in most camps.

In a somewhat lighter vein, yet also important, is the location of the camp's bathroom. "We do have to make sure that everyone uses the same place as an outdoor latrine . . . since, if we are in a tent camp, we also melt the ice and snow for drinking and cooking water, and the two functions don't mix well," noted William Hammer.

Grim reminders of how perilous life can be on Antarctica can be found only 20 miles (32 km) north of McMurdo Station at Camp Evans. First established during Scott's ill-fated expedition, Camp Evans was used again, in 1915, by members of the Ross Sea Party, a team whose mission was to create supply depots for Ernest Shackleton's 1914–1917 Antarctic expedition. Severe weather conditions caused numerous delays to the mission resulting in dangerously depleted food supplies. The party's sled dogs began to die of starvation, some at Camp Evans. The dogs couldn't be buried in the frozen ground so they were left where they fell. Seventy years later, when geologist Reed Scherer visited Camp Evans, he came face-to-face with those dogs. Despite the passage of time, Antarctica's frozen climate had preserved the dogs' bodies. In many places, fur still clung to their skin. The dogs serve as a reminder to everyone: take Happy Camper School seriously.

Left: Robert Falcon Scott's hut at Cape Evans on Ross Island as it was in 2006. To prevent the hut from being buried by glacial ice, conservationists regularly bulldoze ice away from the walls. *Above:* The contents of the hut have been well preserved by Antarctica's frigid climate.

Sleeping out in the field does have its perks. The aurora australis—the South Pole equivalent of the northern lights—illuminates the night sky above a tent near Amundsen-Scott South Pole Station. The small pole to the left of the tent is just a prop—the tent is a little way off from the actual South Pole.

Happy Camper training doesn't focus exclusively on keeping humans safe. Safety of the environment is important too. The scientists must undergo training on how to conduct themselves responsibly with respect to protecting Antarctica's environment and also how to handle the cleanup in case something damaging—an oil spill from a machine, for example—should occur. Not only does this honor the terms of the treaties, but it preserves the pristine condition that makes Antarctica's environment so valuable to scientists.

WHO DOES SCIENCE IN ANTARCTICA?

Many of the scientists who work in Antarctica also teach at colleges and universities around the globe, or they work at laboratories that specialize in scientific research. But there are also special programs that bring elementary, junior high, and high school teachers to Antarctica to work along with the other scientists. It's vital that scientists communicate their research discoveries to people who are not scientists. By visiting Antarctica and immersing themselves in on-going science fieldwork, teachers come to understand the science. As experienced communicators, they can present this knowledge to students and the community at large. In fact, this is so important that in the United States, many of the agencies that fund research in Antarctica require an education outreach plan as part of their application process. Robin Ellwood, who teaches science to eighth graders in New Hampshire, is part of an outreach program. She has joined Earth scientist Peter Doran in four field seasons in Antarctica. Ellwood is a certified master scuba diver, so her underwater diving expertise greatly helps the scientists who are collecting data about freshwater and salt water.

Equipped for the harsh conditions and trained to survive the continent's unique dangers, Ellwood and research scientists manage to do important scientific work year after year on the Antarctic ice. And ice is the most persistent, unavoidable feature of Antarctica. There is no avoiding ice, and yet it is ice that contains Antarctica's most deeply held secrets.

CHAPTER 2

Ice, Ice, and More Ice

THE BASIC FACTS ABOUT ANTARCTIC ICE ASTONISH ALL BY THEMSELVES. The ice that blankets the continent year-round contains almost 90 percent of Earth's freshwater. The total volume of all the ice on the continent is about 6.1 million cubic miles (25 million cu. km). And if all of that ice melted completely, it would raise the global sea level by about 230 feet (70 m). That's enough to flood most of Earth's coastal cities, including New York, Los Angeles, and Tokyo.

The South Pole, often called the bottom of Earth, has always been one of Antarctica's most enticing features. The desire to be first to the South Pole drove many early explorers to test themselves on the ice. And yet the South Pole itself is just ice. The South Pole, located in the central part of the continent, is on an elevated, flat area known as a plateau, more than 9,200 feet (2,800 m) higher than sea level. That's about 1,000 feet (305 m) higher than

A scientist looks out on the ice fields from atop Castle Rock, a large rock formation near McMurdo Station on Ross Island. Robert Falcon Scott first saw Castle Rock on his Discovery Expedition (1901–1904) and named the rock for its shape.

the volcano Mount Saint Helen's, in Washington State. However, if you stood in Antarctica at the South Pole, you wouldn't be standing among rocky mountains. You'd be standing on the surface of a heavy blanket of ice that is about 9,000 feet (2,743 m) thick. When you stand on the bottom of Earth, you stand on top of a layer of ice higher than many mountains.

A FLAKE AT A TIME

The ice didn't just appear. Antarctica is a place where many things happen slowly, including the accumulation of ice. The continent's thick, icy blanket began with light, lacy snowflakes. The drifting snowflake you can catch on your tongue is actually a six-sided crystal of frozen water vapor. All the little open areas inside that lacy snowflake are filled with air. As a matter of fact, a snowflake is 80 percent air. But as soon as a snowflake hits the ground, it begins to change. No longer surrounded by the cold temperatures found high in Earth's atmosphere where the flake formed, parts of the snowflake begin to melt. Water from the melted parts of the flake dribbles toward the snowflake's center and fills some of the air spaces. If the temperature cools, the water refreezes. The flake's edges are no longer crisp, and the air spaces are less well defined. More changes occur if additional snow falls on top of it. The weight of the new snow breaks the snowflake's fragile, weblike structure. The broken snowflakes become more closely packed with other similarly changed snowflakes, just as if you scooped up a handful of snowflakes and packed them into a snowball.

Snow that has lost 50 percent of its air spaces and has lasted at least one summer without completely melting and refreezing as ice is called firn. The word comes from the Swiss dialect of German and means "last year's snow." Snowflakes that have become firn are rounded, with a texture similar to grains of sugar. Firn contains fewer air spaces, although air passages still exist, like tiny tunnels between firn's icy grains.

As seasons pass, new layers of snow squeeze the firn, forcing the individual grains to become locked together until they form a solid mass of ice. At this point, melting and pressure

When a snowflake is viewed through the lens of a microscope, its open air-filled spaces are easily seen.

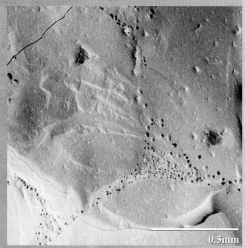

Top: Firn, as seen under a microscope. Note open spaces. *Above:* A microscopic view of glacial ice. Very little room for air remains.

have squeezed most of the air from the ice. The air passages between grains are closed off. Even so, some air does not escape. These small pockets of air remain as bubbles suspended inside the ice—bubbles that contain important clues about Antarctica's past. When firn is squeezed to the point where it contains less than 20 percent air, it is given a new name: glacial ice.

How quickly firn transforms into glacial ice depends on the climate where the firn is. In Alaska, where air and snow temperatures permit partial melting and refreezing to occur frequently and where a lot of new snow falls, firn can become glacial ice in thirty to fifty years. In the interior parts of Antarctica, the same change may take as long as thirty-five hundred years. There are two reasons for this. The first is because the extreme cold found in the areas far from Antarctica's coast prevents snowflakes from melting. The second is that moisture is necessary for snowflakes to form. Regions of the continent far from the coast have little moisture in the air, so new snow seldom falls. The South Pole receives less than 1 inch (2.54 centimeters) of snow per year—as much snow as falls annually in Austin, Texas. Coastal areas, on the other hand, receive 20 to 40 inches (51 to 102 cm) of snow per year, still less than many cities in North America. Averaging all areas together, the continent receives about 2 inches (5 cm) of snow per year.

More than thirty-five million years ago, snowflakes falling on mountaintops all over the continent were the first threads that slowly wove Antarctica's icy blanket. Initially, the snow stayed year-round on only the continent's highest mountains. The snowflakes became firn, which in turn became glacial ice. That glacial ice wedged itself into cracks and crevices on the tops and sides of the mountains. Slowly, relentlessly, the ice picked at the mountains, chipping away slivers of rock, sculpting ever-larger bowl-shaped basins called cirques. More snow and ice filled the cirques. But a cirque, like any bowl, can be filled only so much before it overflows its rim.

That's when big changes began to occur in Antarctica. The pressure created by the buildup of layers forced the glacial ice on Antarctica's mountains to behave in a way very different from the way ice in your freezer behaves. The ice in the cirques began to flow, spilling out onto the sides of the mountains. That's because instead of being brittle and breaking

under pressure like an ice cube crunched by your teeth, enormous pressure causes glacial ice to flow like a very thick liquid, even thicker than honey. As soon as glacial ice starts to move, it is called a glacier. A glacier is a thick, *moving* mass of ice. Pulled downward, away from mountaintops by gravity, glaciers slowly flow toward lower areas. Nothing in a glacier's path is left unchanged. A glacier can wear away mountains and carry boulders that weigh tons. Unless a glacier melts, it will eventually wind its way to the sea, just as rivers do.

The snout, or front edge, of the Hughes Glacier flows toward Lake Bonney in the Taylor Valley.

THE ICE JUST KEPT SPREADING

Over thirty-five million years, the ancient mountain glaciers flowed down the sides of Antarctica's frigid inland mountains and onto the valley floors below. At times, the ice at the front edges of the glaciers melted and the glaciers seemed to retreat back toward the mountaintops. At other times, the glaciers spread farther into the valleys. Eventually, the cycles of spreading and melting reached a tipping point, a time when the glaciers stopped melting and just kept spreading year-round. When they did, the glaciers' icy lobes spilled from their individual valleys and merged with other expanding glaciers, forming ever-larger rivers of ice deep enough to bury hills and valleys. Even as the glaciers combined, new glacial ice from the cirques spilled forth and became part of the ever-spreading, ever-deepening ice. Scientists have created computer programs that are able to simulate this behavior and display it as a video animation.

This photo of the Commonwealth Glacier, which also flows toward the Taylor Valley, shows how two "rivers of ice" merge and create a larger, wider ice floe.

Compressing millions of years of ice movement into a seconds-long video creates a startling overview: the ice seems to pulsate, as though it were Antarctica's beating heart, spreading the ice farther with each beat, until the frozen juggernaut consumed the whole continent. But if you could remove Antarctica's frosty cloak, you would see that a landscape of hills, valleys, and plains still lies below.

A mass of ice that covers a large portion of a continent is called an ice sheet. Antarctica has two such ice sheets. When combined, they spread over an area about 1.4 times the size of the United States. The larger of the two ice sheets is the East Antarctic Ice Sheet. It covers most of the bedrock that forms the continent of Antarctica. The average thickness of this ice sheet is about 7,300 feet (2,226 m). But at its thickest point, the East Antarctic Ice Sheet is 15,665 feet (4,776 m)—almost 3 miles (5 km) thick!

Sizing Up the Ice Sheets

How do geologists know how thick Antarctica's ice sheets are? One tool they use to measure ice depth is called ice-penetrating radar. The same technology police use to catch speeders can be used to measure thickness. Radar uses waves to measure ice depth. The fascinating thing about these waves is that when they come in contact with different kinds of surfaces, the waves slightly change their direction. For example, waves traveling through air move in a straight line. When the waves reach a different substance, like rock, they are reflected off in other directions, and this is the key to using them for measurement.

Taking a measurement with ice-penetrating radar starts high above the ice, in an airplane. Antennas are attached to the tip of each of the plane's wings. As the plane flies over an ice sheet, one antenna sends pulses of waves down through the air to the ice. Some of these waves are reflected by the surface of the ice. Others pass through the ice, but not through the rock that the ice covers. When these waves hit a mass of rock beneath the ice, they reflect back toward the plane. The antenna positioned on the other wing of the plane receives the waves that have been reflected from the ice surface and from the rock. The scientists know exactly how fast the waves travel. Instruments on the plane record the amount of time it takes for a wave to be transmitted from one antenna until the wave is received by the other antenna. From this information, the scientists can calculate the distance from the ice sheet surface to the rock that lies below.

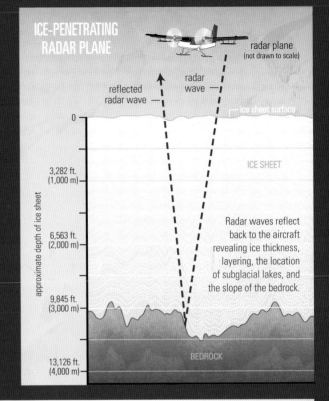

ICE-PENETRATING RADAR PLANE

radar plane (not drawn to scale)

reflected radar wave

radar wave

ice sheet surface

0

ICE SHEET

3,282 ft. (1,000 m)

6,563 ft. (2,000 m)

Radar waves reflect back to the aircraft revealing ice thickness, layering, the location of subglacial lakes, and the slope of the bedrock.

9,845 ft. (3,000 m)

13,126 ft. (4,000 m)

BEDROCK

approximate depth of ice sheet

Working in the field in Antarctica, a technician adjusts the ice-penetrating radar equipment before attaching it to the plane.

The smaller West Antarctic Ice Sheet covers some of the continental bedrock, but it also overlies a number of islands. Large areas of the West Antarctic Ice Sheet rest on bedrock that is as much as 8,200 feet (2,500 m) below sea level. In fact, the base of the West Antarctic Ice Sheet occupies land that otherwise would be the ocean floor.

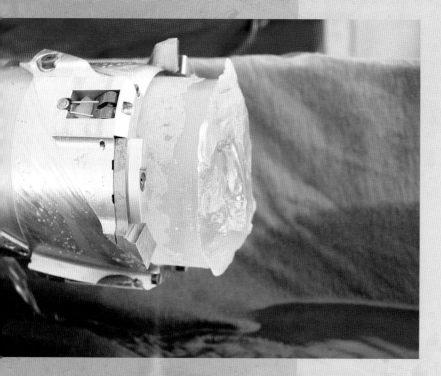

An ice core still in the barrel after the drill has been raised to the surface.

INSIDE THE ICE

A number of snowy summits, called ice domes, rise high above the Antarctic continent as feeders of ice to the Antarctic ice sheets. The ice that forms these domes can extend deeper than 9,800 feet (3,000 m). Many tiny air bubbles that were trapped as the original snow became glacial ice are suspended within those depths, as are dust particles, pieces of ash from volcanic eruptions, and other clues about Antarctica's past climates.

To find the clues, scientists have drilled into the ice sheets and pulled out cores, or cylindrical samples, of the ice. In 2004 scientists participating in the European Project for Ice Coring in Antarctica (EPICA) completed a five-year drilling project into the very deep ice at Dome C, also known as Dome Charlie, located on the Antarctic Plateau, a large elevated area in the central portion of East Antarctica. The drill they used to core Dome C, called a Deep Ice Sheet Coring (DISC) drill, is not like the drill you find on a carpenter's workbench. The electronics of the drill are controlled from a computer on the surface. The cutting end is not a point, like a carpenter's drill bit. Instead, the drill has a hollow, stainless steel tube, or barrel, with cutting blades around the rim on the bottom end. As the cutters spin, they shave a ring-shaped groove into the ice. The solid-ice center ends up being the ice core that goes up inside the barrel. Think of a cookie cutter: the edges of the cookie cutter are like the blades of the cutter. The solid cookie dough that remains is like the ice core. Like the threads on a screw, a spiral on the outside of the barrel carries the ice shavings upward, away from the cutting edge, so the DISC drill can go deeper. As this happens, a second steel tube slips into the ring-shaped cut. It perfectly encases the lengthening ice core and protects it from breaking. When the ice core fills the steel tube, it is snapped off at the bottom. Then the whole barrel and ice core sample are winched back up to the surface. There, the core is cut into shorter lengths and packed in materials that preserve it so the sections can be analyzed in a laboratory. An ice core is typically about 4.8 inches (12 cm) in diameter and is removed from an ice sheet in segments that are almost 9 feet (3 m) long.

A DISC drill has another unusual feature: it injects fluid into the hole as it drills. After all the work of drilling a very deep hole, it may seem surprising to want to fill a hole while you are drilling

A view down the ice-core shaft

it. But it's crucial to do so. That's because without something to replace the ice that has been removed, the pressure of the surrounding ice—which is still moving—would squeeze the hole closed above the drill. The fluid that is injected is specially mixed to be similar to the density of the ice being removed. That equalizes the pressure, and the hole stays open.

In stages, the EPICA team collected an ice core that was 10,728 feet (3,270 m) long— that's more than 2 miles (3 km). As the drill approached the bedrock beneath the dome, the sensors in the drill alerted the team that the ice along the base was melting. The scientists stopped before reaching the melted area because they did not want to risk contaminating the basal layer of water.

Substances found in the ice core, such as volcanic ash, changed the chemistry of the ice and and contained certain elements that enabled the geologists to use scientific instruments to determine the age of the deepest layers contained in the ice core. The ice was at least eight hundred thousand years old! This sample is the oldest ice that has ever been found on Earth thus far.

What else did the ice core tell the scientists? During the past eight hundred thousand years, Earth's climate appears to have changed in a regular pattern of eight warm and cold periods that cycled back and forth about every one hundred thousand years. Right now, we are in the warm part of a cycle.

But what about time periods earlier than eight hundred thousand years ago? On Dome C, that remains a mystery for now, at least. The tremendous weight of the ice dome squeezed, bent, and twisted the ice layers closest to the base of Dome C—so much so that some of them were folded like a blanket that's been scrunched up at the foot of a bed. The geologists could see the folded layers in the ice core. Also, the heat at the base of thick ice causes some layers to melt and become indistinguishable. Together, these conditions made it impossible for scientists to interpret any climatic information earlier than eight hundred thousand years ago.

Hopes are high that another dome on the continent will provide an ice core that could be as old as 1.4 million years. Dome A—which stands for Argus—rises 13,431 feet (4,094 m) above sea level. Its location, miles from the closest research station, and its high altitude make Dome A an extremely inhospitable place to work. Simply walking at this altitude requires considerable effort. Nevertheless, in February 2009, the Kunlun Station, named after the Kunlun Mountains in western China, was officially opened. Its construction was not an easy task considering that at times the temperature was −47°F (−44°C). More equipment for conducting experiments and also for sustaining human life will be installed in the coming years, with hopes of drilling an ice core into Dome A by the 2012 field season. While the station is operated by the Chinese government, the drilling itself is likely to be a multinational project.

Researcher Paolo Gabrielli carefully removes a core sample from the cold storage facility at Ohio State University's Byrd Polar Research Center in Ohio. The center is home to one of the largest collections of ice core samples in the world.

ICE ON THE MOVE

People often use the word *frozen* to describe something that is stuck in place. One of Antarctica's frozen secrets—a secret that is true of glaciers everywhere—is that "frozen" glacial ice actually moves in several different ways, sometimes at once.

Even though the East and West Antarctic ice sheets are immense and very thick, they are really just gigantic glaciers, slowly sliding over the bedrock that lies beneath them. However, if you were to watch the surface of the ice, you couldn't actually see the ice moving. But it is. Deep at the base of an ice sheet, geothermal heat from inside Earth and pressure from the weight of the glacier melt some of the ice at the bottom of the ice sheet. Water that melts from glacial ice is called meltwater. When meltwater collects underneath a glacier, it acts as a lubricant between the ice and the bedrock, making it easier for glacial ice to slide across the land.

In addition to sliding along its base—what scientists call basal sliding—glacial ice simultaneously moves in a second way within the body of the glacier. These movements are caused by the enormous pressure created by numerous layers of ice. The tremendous weight of the ice forces individual ice crystals within the glacier to line up in such a way that they slide against one another. These very small, continuous movements allow the ice to bend and flow like honey. Through basal sliding and ice crystals slipping and sliding inside the continent's glaciers, Antarctica's ice sheets act like gigantic conveyer belts, slowly carrying ice from the continent's inner regions out toward the coast.

As glaciers flow, they often form intriguing features within the ice. For instance, sometimes channels of ice form within an ice sheet. These channels, called ice streams, are like rivers flowing within the ice sheet. Ice streams flow faster than the ice that surrounds them. And this fact has grabbed the attention of researchers who have identified a number of ice streams in Antarctica. The West Antarctic Ice Sheet has two networks of ice streams. These two networks feed new ice onto two large, flat areas in western Antarctica called the Ross and the Ronne-Filchner ice shelves. Some of the ice streams in these networks flow hundreds of yards a year, a distance farther and faster than many smaller glaciers move in the same time span.

Measuring how far and how fast an ice stream moves isn't an easy task. But scientists can do it by combining the information gleaned from ice-penetrating radar with additional data collected with another scientific instrument called a seismograph.

A seismograph records seismic waves, typically the waves of energy produced by an earthquake. Seismic waves travel through both ice and rock, but their speed changes when they pass from ice into rock. How quickly the waves move through the two substances is recorded with a seismograph. Among other things, this data helps scientists create images of the ground that lies beneath Antarctica's snow-mantled icy surface. However, geologists don't have to wait for an earthquake to get seismic waves. They can create their own seismic waves with instruments that cause the ground to shake, like a mini, manmade earthquake. A seismograph records these vibrations as if they were an actual earthquake.

Seismographs sometimes show scientists things they weren't looking for, especially in Antarctica. During the Antarctic summers of 2001 to 2003, geologist Douglas Wiens and his colleagues made many observations of the ice and its behavior. However, the most surprising discovery didn't occur until they were back in their laboratory at Washington University, in Saint Louis. While they were analyzing data collected by seismographs located in the Transantarctic Mountains, they noticed a series of perplexing seismic waves. No natural earthquakes had occurred nor had any scientists created any earthquakes at the times the waves were recorded. Further investigation helped Wiens's team pinpoint the mystifying waves to the Whillans Ice Stream, which was 500 miles (805 km) away from the area where the team had been working. Even more puzzling, the seismic waves seemed to be coming from the ice.

Inexplicably, the seismographs indicated that the Whillans Ice Stream, which is 60 miles (97 km) wide and about half a mile (0.8 km) deep, was producing seismic waves similar to those produced by an earthquake. Wiens's team was determined to discover what was happening. Usually, the Whillans moves slowly, about 3 feet (0.9 m) per day. Further observation of the seismic data revealed that the Whillans Ice Stream wasn't moving steadily. Instead, it stuttered in a regular pattern of stops and starts. The ice flowed for ten minutes, slipping forward about 18 inches (46 cm) during that time period. Then all movement ceased for twelve hours, after which the ice moved again for ten minutes, again sliding forward about 18 inches. The mysterious waves that the seismographs had recorded were energy waves produced by ice movements. Geologists are very familiar with this kind of movement but in another scenario. Rock in an earthquake zone often moves in this fashion—although the ground movement during an earthquake lasts a much shorter period of time, often only seconds. This stop-and-start motion is frequently called a stick-slip motion, and it's controlled by friction.

Patrick Shore, a member of Wiens's team, installs seismograph equipment at Cape Roberts, near the Transantarctic Mountains. The instrument supplied data about movement of the Whillans Ice Stream.

Researcher Tim Parker carefully installs and levels a sensor that monitors seismic waves in a hole dug in the snow.

"The base of the ice stream is right along the boundary between the ice sheet and the soil or bedrock. The ice is about half a mile [0.8 km] thick," Wiens explained.

His team realized that one constant spot in the ice stream always seemed to get stuck. Friction within the ice sheet would hold the ice in this spot in place. As it did, pressure began building up in the area of the stuck ice. (The pressure builds because the surrounding ice is still sliding; it pushes and pulls on the stuck ice.) Eventually, the stress became stronger than the ice could bear, and the stuck ice would suddenly break loose from the sticking point and slip 18 inches (46 cm) forward. When an earthquake shifts rock with a stick-slip motion, the brittle rock on Earth's surface often cracks. Because glacial ice is less brittle, the Whillans's stick-slip motion does not create surface cracks in the ice. The movement differs from an earthquake in another way: when an earthquake occurs, you can feel the ground shake. "If you stand on the Whillans Ice Stream during one of the slip events you do not feel it," noted Wiens, "There have been field camps on the Whillans Ice Stream several times and nobody noticed the slip events."

Wondering why the ice stream moved in this peculiar fashion, Wiens's team examined the base of the Whillans. "A radar survey showed that the sticking spot is dryer than other areas," Wiens said. The meltwater may be lubricating the ice stream elsewhere, allowing it to slip easily in those areas. "Another possibility is that the sticky spot represents a place where ice slides across bare rock, whereas in other places it slides across soil or ground up rock," he continued. Unlike bedrock, soil and sediment do not hold fast in place.

Before this discovery, scientists had not known that ice streams could move regularly in a stick-slip manner. So far, the Whillans is the only ice stream where this pattern has been observed. "We hope to find some more cases of this kind of stick-slip behavior so we can better understand the cause," Wiens added.

The area where the Whillans Ice Stream begins receives about 8 inches (20 cm) of compacted new snow each year. In this area, the Whillans does not move with the stick-slip motion. It only flows in the usual creeping fashion of other glaciers. As the ice stream nears the Ross Ice Shelf, however, the Whillans flows in three ways: with basal sliding, with the honeylike flow caused by pressure, and with the stick-slip flow. Close to the Ross Sea, almost all the motion occurs in the stick-slip form. As of fall 2008, a Global Positioning System (GPS) receiver that some of Wiens's colleagues installed near the Whillans indicated that the stick-slip motion continues.

One thing the team has observed about the Whillans is that the surface of the ice stream is decreasing in elevation. "This is because the ice stream is carrying away more ice than is produced by new snowfall," Wiens explained. "But we don't know if this is a long-term situation. The motion rate of the Whillans is decreasing. It may eventually even stop. We would really like to know what is controlling the changing motion rates of the ice streams, as this will be very important for understanding the future of the West Antarctic Ice Sheet." Even as Wiens monitors what's happening on the Whillans, a massive five-year project called WISSARD (Whillans Ice Stream Subglacial Access Research Drilling) is now under way to study not only the Whillans and the water beneath it but also how its icy flow adds to the Ross Ice Shelf. After ice from the Whillans is incorporated into the ice shelf, it comes in contact with the ocean. In this area, any melting that occurs could affect the stability of the West Antarctic Ice Sheet. Another part of the WISSARD project will be investigating what kind of life, if any, might be living inside and beneath the ice stream. WISSARD'S first ice-drilling expedition is scheduled for the 2010–2011 field season.

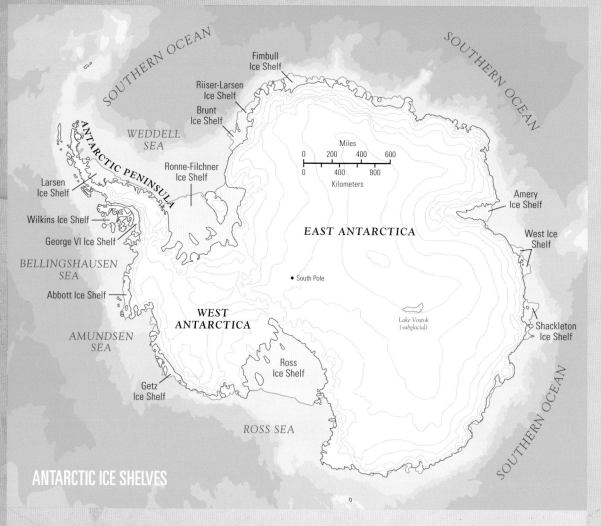

More than a dozen ice shelves fringe the Antarctic coastline.

SOUTHERN OCEAN

SOUTHERN OCEAN

Fimbull Ice Shelf

Riiser-Larsen Ice Shelf

Brunt Ice Shelf

WEDDELL SEA

Ronne-Filchner Ice Shelf

Larsen Ice Shelf

ANTARCTIC PENINSULA

Wilkins Ice Shelf

George VI Ice Shelf

BELLINGSHAUSEN SEA

Abbott Ice Shelf

AMUNDSEN SEA

Getz Ice Shelf

WEST ANTARCTICA

Ross Ice Shelf

ROSS SEA

EAST ANTARCTICA

• South Pole

Lake Vostok (subglacial)

Amery Ice Shelf

West Ice Shelf

Shackleton Ice Shelf

SOUTHERN OCEAN

Miles
0   200   400   600
0   400   800
Kilometers

ANTARCTIC ICE SHELVES

Although scientists are studying all areas of Antarctica's ice sheets, they are most carefully watching those bodies of ice that reach the continent's coastline. In these places, the ice sheets push out into the ocean, advancing into the sea, where they may create huge, floating shelves of ice. Why are these particular secrets worth knowing? Remember: enough water is frozen in Antarctica that were it all to thaw, it would submerge many of Earth's coastal cities. Smaller changes in the behavior of Antarctic ice can also create dramatic changes around the globe. Understanding the ways ice moves on Antarctica can help scientists predict what will happen to coastlines throughout the world, affecting millions of lives.

FLOATING ICE

Sea ice—floating chunks and land-anchored ice shelves—can change the whole "look" of Antarctica. During the summer, separate chunks of sea ice clutter the water. Waves raise and lower the close but freely moving pieces in an undulating rhythm like muscles rippling beneath an animal's skin. In winter, however, the free-floating pieces freeze fast to the ice shelves, doubling the area of the continent.

How does an ice shelf like the Ross, which exists year-round, form? Formation starts when the advancing edge, or front, of an ice sheet reaches the sea. However, the glaciers farther inland don't stop flowing. They keep feeding more ice into the ice sheet, which in turn pushes the front into the sea. The ice sheet inches seaward, pushing the water aside and covering the seafloor. Because ice is less dense than seawater, the seaward edge begins to float. Seawater seeps beneath the ice sheet, raising it off the seafloor. At this point, it becomes a thick, floating shelf made of ice.

Antarctic ice has many different textures. It also forms eye-catching patterns. This floating ice, called pancake ice, covers large areas of the Bellingshausen Sea.

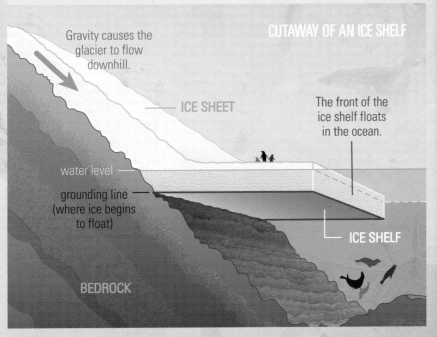

CUTAWAY OF AN ICE SHELF

Gravity causes the glacier to flow downhill.

ICE SHEET

The front of the ice shelf floats in the ocean.

water level

grounding line (where ice begins to float)

ICE SHELF

BEDROCK

Ross Island with Mount Erebus in the background. Mount Erebus is the southernmost active volcano on Earth. The white cliffs are the front edge of an ice shelf.

The landward side, or the rear of the ice shelf, remains connected to the land, from which glacial ice supplies a continuing flow of new ice to the ice shelf. Ice sheets flow more rapidly over the sea than they do over bedrock because there is much less friction beneath the floating ice.

Most of the East Antarctic Ice Sheet lies on top of bedrock with a number of ice shelves fringing its coastline. But the ice shelves along East Antarctica's coast are small when compared to those that form along the West Antarctic Ice Sheet. That's because the seafloor, rather than bedrock, underlies many areas of the West Antarctic Ice Sheet. Earth's largest ice shelf, the Ross Ice Shelf, extends from the West Antarctic Ice Sheet all the way to the southern ranges of the Transantarctic Mountains, covering an area about the size of France. The front of the Ross Ice Shelf towers straight up from the sea, forming sheer ice cliffs that range from 48 to 164 feet (15 to 50 m) above sea level. These measurements scarcely reflect the ice shelf's thickness: 90 percent of the ice shelf's mass lies hidden beneath the sea's surface. Like other ice shelves, the Ross Ice Shelf receives a steady supply of new ice from the ice sheet and from smaller glaciers that have reached the coastal area. Also like other ice shelves, the Ross Ice Shelf loses ice when pieces along the edge break off, becoming huge chunks of floating ice called icebergs. Scientists call this calving. The largest iceberg ever recorded calved off the Ross Ice Shelf in March 2000.

This colossal iceberg, which scientists named B-15, was 183 miles (295 km) long and 23 miles (37 km) wide—only a little smaller than the state of Connecticut! Since then, B-15 has broken apart, creating a number of smaller—but still good-sized—icebergs.

Just as scientists want to understand how glacial ice moves farther up the ice sheets, they also want to know the rates at which ice calves from the ice shelves and into the sea. All of these frozen phenomena are factors in maintaining balance throughout Earth's oceans. Scientists hope to learn enough about the delicate balance before the oceans reach a point where significant change to the ice sheet will be irreversible.

Steep cliffs formed the edges of the massive iceberg B-15. At the time this photo was taken, the iceberg was 90 miles (145 km) long and was floating near Ross Island, Antarctica.

CHAPTER 3

Beneath the Ice

ANTARCTICA IS KNOWN FIRST AND FOREMOST FOR ITS ICY COVERING, AN EVER-CHANGING FACE WITH MANY MOODS. But it is more than a continent-sized chunk of ice. Craggy mountaintops poke through, and many places near the coast on the Antarctic Peninsula are free of ice in the summer. So we know rock lies beneath the icy blanket. For many years, geologists wanted to know more about that hidden bedrock. The trick was finding ways to look at it.

MAPPING THE WORLD BENEATH THE ICE

Traveling on Antarctica's frozen, wind-raked surface is hard enough. Seeing through that surface, through thousands of feet of ice, to the bedrock below seems like an impossible task. Fortunately, science has a way around this problem. Technologies like ice-penetrating radar and seismographs, which can measure the thickness of ice, also provide the information that geologists need to create a picture of Antarctica's surface stripped of its icy blanket.

The peaks of the Transantarctic Mountains poke through the ice.

By knowing the distances the radar and seismic waves travel and the time it takes to do so, geologists can calculate the depth of the ice. In some places, the waves from ice-penetrating radar and seismographs only traveled a short distance before being reflected. This told geologists that the ice sheet in those areas was not as thick. In other places, the waves traveled deeply before they hit bedrock. That meant the ice sheet in those areas was very thick. As geologists mapped how shallow or deep the ice was, it also revealed how high or low the bedrock beneath the ice was.

Geologists from many countries have collected information about the depth of the ice sheets in different places around the continent. However, the information hadn't been combined in a way that could be used to create a complete map of the bedrock that formed the whole continent. To remedy that situation, scientists once again came together across national boundaries and cooperated. In 1996 the Scientific Committee on Antarctic Research, an organization that develops and monitors international research in Antarctica, sponsored a project called BEDMAP (short for Antarctic BEDrock MAPping). Scientists from eight different countries took part. Their plan was to encourage all scientists who had measured ice thicknesses anywhere in Antarctica to pool their information. When they combined these measurements, a picture emerged of Antarctica's land surface stripped of ice. What the geologists found was fascinating: many mountains and valleys lie hidden beneath Antarctica's ice sheets.

HITTING BEDROCK

The contours of the rock beneath the Antarctic ice sheets are only part of the story of Antarctic rock. More details unfolded when scientists applied a familiar technique to Antarctica's bedrock: core sampling. Sediment and rock cores enable geologists to look at Antarctic history much more ancient than what can be recorded in ice cores. Geologists

ELEVATION

	13,120 ft. (4,000 m)
	9,840 ft. (3,000 m)
	6,560 ft. (2,000 m)
	3,280 ft. (1,000 m)
	0
	-3,280 ft. (-1,000 m)
	-6,560 ft. (-2,000 m)
	-9,840 ft. (-3,000 m)
	-13,120 ft. (-4,000 m)
	-16,400 ft. (-5,000 m)
	-19,680 ft. (-6,000 m)

This map shows the elevations of Antarctica's land surfaces as they would appear if all the ice were stripped away. It is one of the fruits of BEDMAP's labors. The project is only one example of what scientists can accomplish when nations cooperate.

A metal drain pipe, the kind used to channel storm waters on less icy continents, has been frozen into the ice, where it becomes the rigid wall of ANDRILL's drill shaft. Deep down in the core, the drill hole is kept open with hot water that is pumped down the shaft through the black hose on the left side of the shaft.

collect rock cores by drilling into the bedrock beneath the ice shelves that are at the edge of the ice sheet. A group of more than two hundred scientists from Germany, Italy, New Zealand, Great Britain, and the United States participate in a drilling program called Antarctic Geological Drilling (ANDRILL). Their goal is to learn more about how Antarctica's climate has changed over the course of millions of years and how the present icy conditions were established. This information may help them predict how changes in climate are likely to affect Antarctica—and Earth—in the future.

The sediments ANDRILL scientists have examined so far come from two cores. One was drilled beneath the McMurdo Ice Shelf, which is the northwestern part of the Ross Island Shelf, near Ross Island. The other core was drilled from the seafloor beneath nearby McMurdo Sound.

Ross Powell is an ANDRILL geologist who has examined the sediment core drilled beneath the McMurdo Ice Shelf. As Powell explained, drilling a sediment core is very different from drilling an ice core. "The drill bit we use to cut our cores has industrial diamonds embedded in it so it can grind through rock. . . . We start off with a diameter of about 2.5 inches [6 cm] and end with one about 1 inch [2.5 cm]. The diameter changes with depth because the deeper you go, the more steel pipe you use to obtain the core. So to cut down on the weight, we use narrower pipe," Powell stated. "The lengths of the core recovered vary from 10 to 29 feet [3 to 9 m], depending on the quality of the rock. Good rock gets 29 foot runs." When a core section reaches the surface, it is cut into 1-yard (1 m) lengths. It is then labeled and wrapped for storage and further analysis.

Powell finds the rock cores drilled by ANDRILL fascinating for a couple of reasons. "The ice cores from other areas can tell us about atmospheric conditions in the past. . . . But they can't really tell us about the size of the ice sheet in the past," Powell explained. "That's because ice core information only goes back 800,000 years in time. Sediment cores contain materials that are millions of years older than the ice. And those materials can tell us about the size of the ice sheet."

The sediments that lie on the bottom of a body of water accumulate in layers, and these layers can tell scientists much about how a place changes over time. This kind of scientific examination has a name, *stratigraphy*, from the Latin word *strata*, which means "layers." Stratigraphy is a special branch of geology that studies the order in which layers of sediment or rock are formed. When scientists talk about a particular area's stratigraphy, they are talking about the layers of material found in its soil, rock, or ice. Plant and animal remains that are included in those layers become part of the stratigraphy.

How can sediments tell us about an ice sheet's size and behavior, especially if those changes occurred many millions of years ago? The stratigraphy of the sediments in the McMurdo Ice Shelf core gave Powell and his colleagues the clues they needed to answer this question. First, the core's layers told them the order in which various sediment layers were deposited. Unless the layers have been pushed out of place, the oldest layers are always at the bottom. Next, the layers collected by the core are formed of different types of sedimentary rock. Each type of sedimentary rock has distinctive characteristics that allow geologists to determine the kinds of environmental conditions—including the position of the ice sheet—that existed at the time the layers of sediments accumulated. Scientists also analyze samples of the core for the amount of certain elements contained in the sediments. Calculations made from these findings revealed that the deepest, and therefore oldest, sediments in the core that Powell examined are about thirteen and a half million years old.

"The sediment record from both ANDRILL cores tells us when the West Antarctic Ice Sheet was right above the places we drilled. The cores tell us when the edge of the ice sheet had moved away from the drilling sites but still extended over the sea and produced icebergs. And it tells us when the West Antarctic Ice Sheet had pulled back away from the water completely, in other words, when it got smaller," Powell stated.

The sediment layers in the ANDRILL cores occurred in alternating patterns throughout the core. Some of the layers contained sediments that are only deposited in marine environments. That meant the ocean must have flooded the area at that time. Others contained the kinds of sediment layers that form in a freshwater environment. In these layers, the water that deposited the sediments was meltwater from the ice sheet.

The stratigraphy of these sediment layers tells a three million year old story of ice sheet movement.

The fine-grained sediment layers in the uppermost section were deposited in a marine environment. Remains of certain kinds of marine algae that live in freely flowing, warmer ocean water were found in these sediments.

Layers in the longer middle section were deposited just in front of the ice, as the ice sheet melted and receded.

The sediment layers in the bottommost section were deposited when ice completely covered the area.

During these times, ice, rather than ocean, engulfed the area. "How those layers stacked up vertically in the sediment cores told us about the ice sheet's ancient movement. You've basically got a time machine that as it transports you deeper below the sea floor, also takes you back in time, showing that the ice sheet was moving back and forth over the drilling sites throughout its history," said Powell. At times the area was buried beneath ice, and at others it was flooded by open sea.

ANDRILL scientists have used computers to create a model that simulates how Antarctica's current icy state evolved. In a time-lapse sequence, glaciers first began on high mountaintops. They grew and shrunk, each time spreading a bit farther and covering more land before retreating. Finally, the ice extends far enough that it reaches a tipping point beyond which the ice no longer melts. It just keeps spreading until it reaches the current levels.

As work continues in Antarctica, ice and sediment cores will continue to provide more information about Antarctica's ancient climates. In the meantime, scientists are eagerly exploring some places where bedrock—and the secrets it contains—is exposed at the surface.

DOWN IN THE VALLEYS

It doesn't always take a massive drill to get to Antarctica's bedrock. Several of Antarctica's valleys are not filled with ice. Because these valleys are more accessible, it's easier for geologists to study the rocks and soil and for biologists to study any living organisms that might be found.

Just east of the Transantarctic Mountains, a series of ice-free valleys stretch toward the coast. The valleys in this area are called the Dry Valleys—so called because the Transantarctic Mountains act like a dam that prevents the East Antarctic Ice Sheet from flowing into them.

In Antarctica, scientists are working in an environment unchanged by human activity. This is especially true in the

Members of a research team from Montana State University carry water samples from Lake Bonney to camp.

Dry Valleys, where some areas support life, a rarity on inland Antarctica. The life-forms in the Dry Valleys—plants, microbes, and insects—eke out their existence under delicately balanced conditions. The scientists who work in these valleys have an opportunity to study life under conditions unlike those anywhere else on Earth, but they also must take extra care not to damage the ecosystem.

WATER IN THE DRY VALLEYS

Lakes are one of the remarkable features found in the Dry Valleys. Unlike lakes on other continents, the lakes on Antarctica's surface are capped year-round with ice thick enough

Mount J. J. Thomson overlooking the Taylor Valley—one of the Dry Valleys. In midsummer the sun never sets on Antarctica. This photo was taken at one in the morning.

The cracked and windswept surface of Lake Bonney

to walk on. Also, unlike other lakes, the surface of these lakes is not the smooth, slick ice that ice-skaters enjoy. Scoured by wind and pitted by rocks and chunks of ice, ridges and dips—like an old washboard—cover the surface of Antarctica's lakes. One of these lakes, Lake Vanda, is located in the middle of Wright Valley, and the lake has some remarkable features.

Lake Vanda is about 5 miles long (8 km). At its deepest point, it is about 250 feet (76 m) deep. Except for the small amount of water along the edge during the summer, the lake's surface is permanently topped with 11.5 feet (3.5 m) of ice. But beneath the ice, the water temperature is surprisingly warm. Near the bottom of the lake, the water temperature averages 77°F (25°C). That's about the temperature of a warm swimming pool! As strange as it may seem, it's the thick layer of ice that helps keep the water so warm. In the summer, nearly round-the-clock sunlight penetrates through the ice, heating the water below. During the winter, the ice becomes a layer of insulation that stops the heat from escaping.

Lake Vanda and other lakes in the region are somewhat unusual in that they are saltwater lakes. That's because when freshwater evaporates in the Dry Valleys, chemical changes cause the water to become salty.

A group of scientists led by Peter Doran have eagerly turned their attention to another salty lake located in Taylor Valley, the valley next to Wright Valley.

Lake Bonney is 4.3 miles (7 km) long and a little more than half a mile (1 km) wide. An underwater ridge divides the lake into two sections: a smaller western lobe (West Lake Bonney) that ends at Taylor Glacier and a longer eastern lobe (East Lake Bonney). At their deepest points, both lobes are about 130 feet (40 m) deep. Like Lake Vanda, Lake Bonney is permanently ice-covered. Protected from fierce Antarctic winds, the water in Lake Bonney is still and quiet. As with Lake Vanda, the water at the bottom of the lake is salty—five times saltier than seawater.

"The west lobe of Lake Bonney receives freshwater from Taylor Glacier. This water is much lighter than the salty bottom water," explains Peter Doran. Because the freshwater is less dense, "it remains on the surface and it is the water that will evaporate and leave the lake first. For all intents and purposes, the lake is stagnant." As a result, it's likely that the water at the bottom of the lake has been there for a very long time. That means it may hold clues that could help scientists understand how the lake has changed over time.

DIVE!

Sometimes, the only way to gather information is to dive into the water. Scuba diving in Antarctica requires precautions not needed in warm areas. The rubber wet suits that scuba divers typically wear are not enough for Antarctica. The frigid water would quickly draw the diver's body heat through the rubber suit. If the heat in the core of a person's body—the portion of the body that contains the lungs, the heart, the stomach, and the liver—is lowered by more than a few degrees, the person suffers injury and could die. Divers in Antarctica, therefore, dress accordingly.

Even with the protection of special dry suits, Antarctic diving is a frigid proposition. A thermos of hot water is kept at hand to melt ice that forms on diving equipment.

Ian Hawes helps diver Robin Ellwood adjust her face mask prior to entering a lake. The large watch on her left wrist tells Ellwood how much time she's been underwater. If she is using scuba tanks, she can calculate how many minutes of air remain in the tanks.

"We don't wear wet suits. We use dry suits. These suits allow you to wear any clothing you want under them because your body is kept dry," explained Doran. A dry suit is made of heavy, waterproof rubber that traps air next to the body, and that air provides insulation.

Divers breathe underwater in two ways. When diving in Antarctica's ocean waters, divers use self-contained underwater breathing apparatus, usually called scuba gear. This is what recreational divers around the world use. Scuba gear consists of tanks filled with compressed air that are strapped onto a diver's back. Hoses and a mouthpiece carry air to the diver, who wears a face mask and an insulated hood to prevent loss of body heat through the scalp. Since the water temperature can be 28°F (–2°C), a diver may wear a face mask that covers the cheeks, the nose, and the lips. Gloves, at times two- or three-layered pairs, complete the outfit.

Scuba diving in the sea around Antarctica is a unique experience, even for a master diver like junior high teacher Robin Ellwood. She says scuba divers in Antarctica hear a wide variety of underwater sounds depending on where they are diving. "Under the sea ice, other ice floes bump and grind against other ice as they all shift around," Ellwood explained. "It can be quite eerie sounding. At times it sounds like metal grinding up against other chunks of metal. At other times it sounds like Styrofoam squeaking, and at still other times it sounds like trees rubbing against each other in a gentle breeze in the woods!" It can also be frightening, as Ellwood attested. "When the ice cracks, it can sound like massive thunder rolls that seem to go on forever. If it is a serious cracking in the ice, it literally sounds like cannon shots. I have been startled by more than one 'explosion!' One time, I literally ducked while I was diving—pulled my hands up over my head and waited for things to come crashing down on me. I laughed after a moment and relaxed as I remembered that even if the ice did completely shatter and break apart, it would still float. It wasn't going to crash down on me. Funny how our minds work." The ocean surrounding Antarctica teems with many large life-forms, including several species of seals. Divers can hear the underwater sounds that the seals make. "I LOVE listening to the seals. The Weddell seals make the most beautiful sounds, such as singing, chirping, and clicking. Out of the water, I have stood on sea ice and been able to hear the seals singing to each other right through the ice!" Ellwood said.

When divers work underwater in the lakes in the Dry Valleys, they often rely on a continuous surface supply of air rather than scuba gear. For these dives, they wear a helmet rather than use scuba gear. "The helmet covers the entire head, so we stay relatively dry—in most cases completely dry. The air is pumped to the diver's helmet through a tether from the surface supply," Ellwood explained.

The air hose to the diver's helmet also acts as a tether to the hole in the ice. It is literally the diver's lifeline, so for safety reasons, the tether is attached to the helmet and is also snapped to the diver's belt. "If the tether breaks, we would have no air supply. So we make sure it can't break," Doran noted. The tether also contains a communications cable that allows the diver to talk with team members on the surface. In addition to being the main air supply and communications line, there's another reason why the team makes sure the line is securely attached to the diver and unbreakable. "The tether is the path back to the hole," Ellwood explained. "In Antarctic lakes, the dive hole quickly blends into the ice overhead, so it's very hard to actually see the hole until you get fairly close."

If the tether became detached, the diver might not be able to find the hole in the ice where he or she entered the lake. "The ice is 15 feet [5 m] thick so there is no way to break through it if you're away from the hole," Doran stated.

Although divers have a secure tether and a constant supply of surface air, it's always smart to have a plan B in Antarctica. "The diver does take a pony bottle—a small extra container of air—on his or her back, which has an air supply of 5 to 15 minutes. This pony bottle can be turned on by the diver using a valve at the helmet if it

Robin Ellwood gives the OK sign as she prepares to dive using a continuous surface supply of air. The air hose, tether, and communications cables are visible to her right.

is needed in an emergency," Robin Ellwood said. Dives don't usually last more than about an hour. By then, the diver's hands are too cold to continue working. Even after leaving the water, divers can't immediately shake off the cold. "It's challenging to warm up after diving below the ice. We huddle around the stove in the dive hut—sometimes lying with our feet up in the air next to the stove in order to hurry warmth back into our toes," Ellwood added.

What's it like to swim beneath a thick layer of lake ice? Sometimes, especially after one of the region's rare snowfalls, it may be dark. But unless the team is examining a feature in great detail, "Most of the time we don't use lights. There's usually enough sunlight getting through the ice to operate without them," Doran explained. A lack of sunlight doesn't concern Doran's team because in Antarctica the sun doesn't set all summer, from the end of October until the end of February. Diving in a lake is also quieter than diving in the ocean. The chatter of large animals like seals is absent. "Antarctic lakes have only microscopic life-forms, so the underwater sounds are just those made by diving gear and ice creaking, cracking, and moaning. However, breathing inside the helmet seems noisier than in scuba gear—I feel like Darth Vader when I'm using the dive helmet. To hear subtle ice sounds, I need to breathe quietly," said Ellwood.

During past expeditions at Lake Bonney, Doran's divers have collected sediment from the lake and they've sampled the water. They also collected samples of the microscopic organisms that live in the lake. These microbes thrive in an isolated environment where the temperature is permanently cold and it's always dark. Sunlight doesn't provide these creatures with the energy they need to survive. Instead, they sustain themselves on chemical energy. This energy comes from chemical reactions that occur when the freshwater melting from Taylor Glacier mixes with the ancient remnants of the environment that existed in the area millions of years ago. Chemical elements from that environment are in the slushy ice that discharges from the bottom of Taylor Glacier. The data and samples the team collects are analyzed in laboratories at the end of the fieldwork season. As they do so, the team members hope this information, along with additional data that they plan to collect in the future, will provide insight into how the ancient environment changed over time, giving rise to the conditions that support the lake's existing life-forms.

A ROBOT JOINS THE TEAM

During the 2008–2009 field season, Doran's team explored West Lake Bonney in another way: with the help of an autonomous underwater vehicle (AUV), an underwater robot. The new robotic team member had a two-part mission. First, the robot would collect data that would be used to create maps of the lake's basin. The maps would be useful to future research at the lake. The second part of the AUV's mission was to help scientists learn how they might improve the technology of AUVs. They want to do so because an AUV is similar to the type of equipment that scientists hope to use to explore Europa, one of the planet Jupiter's moons. An AUV could travel beneath the moon's ice-covered ocean, searching for life-forms. Exploring an extreme environment like that of Lake Bonney would give the AUV a rigorous test and reveal what kinds of improvements might be needed. Also, the team would gain valuable experience in how to deal with surprises—the glitches that almost always occur when testing new technologies in the field.

The team's AUV is called ENDURANCE, a name derived by shortening the words "Environmentally Non-Disturbing Under-ice Robotic ANtarctiC Explorer." Not coincidentally, it was also the name of Antarctic explorer Ernest Shackleton's ship on the 1914 Imperial Trans-Antarctic Expedition (scientists working on Antarctica have a strong sense of history). By 2008 ENDURANCE had passed underwater tests in the United States and was ready to explore West Lake Bonney.

Even though no people are inside ENDURANCE, they must be present on the surface to monitor its location and the information sent by its computer system, which is connected to the surface by a fiber-optic cable. "It requires five to six full-time engineers and computer people to operate it" said Peter Doran. So it

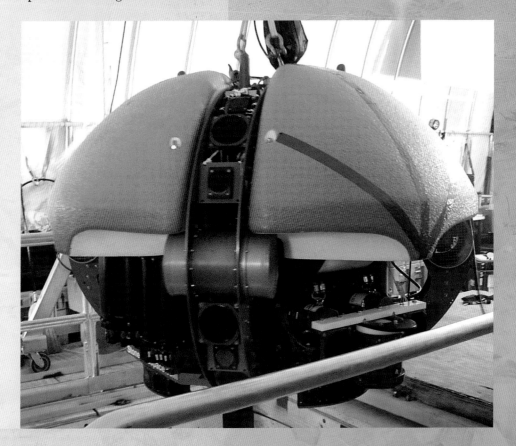

The AUV ENDURANCE awaits its next mission.

On shore, engineers monitor the ENDURANCE with computers connected to ENDURANCE by fiber-optic cable.

was important that technicians and engineers from Stone Aerospace, the company that manufactured ENDURANCE, be members of the team. Should ENDURANCE—usually called "the bot" by the team—malfunction, they would be on hand to help fix it.

Taking ENDURANCE to Lake Bonney and getting it set up was a project in itself, requiring a number of helicopter trips. The bot can't be transported completely assembled because many of its parts are fragile, especially the sonde, the piece of equipment that contains sensitive scientific instruments used to gather data from the lake. The sensors in these instruments measure a number of different characteristics of the lake's water including temperature, the amount of sunlight that filters through the water, and whether the water contains a lot of acid. Other sensors measure the amounts of chlorophyll (the substance that gives green color to plants and certain bacteria) and decayed material from organisms such as bacteria that are present in the water. All of these instruments can be easily damaged if jarred. So a helicopter carried the unassembled (and safely packed) parts of ENDURANCE to the lake in a sling suspended from the helicopter. But before assembling the bot, the team had to build the Bot House on West Lake Bonney. The bot and the equipment needed to operate it require a large, weatherproof shelter with electricity. Essentially, the team needed to build a small barn on a lake in Antarctica. They were up for the task, but it wasn't easy.

Before heading to Lake Bonney, the team had conducted a trial setup of the Bot House at McMurdo Station to be sure everything would still fit together properly after being exposed to cold weather. Nevertheless, it wasn't only the cold that created problems during the trial setup. In her expedition blog, as she described the trial setup, Ellwood wrote, "There were a few moments today when I suspected if we just held on tight to the tent lines that were being used to secure the tent cover in place that the wind would allow the entire team to parasail over to Lake Bonney!" Despite the gusts, the team managed to set the Bot House up in about six hours. During the next few days, the team repacked the Bot House and everyone prepared to leave for Lake Bonney—everyone but Robin Ellwood. "Weather Rules" is the number one guideline in Antarctica. Earlier weather-related delays in getting the bot to Antarctica had put the team behind schedule, just long enough to put a crimp in Ellwood's own schedule, which required her to return to the United States. So, much as she hoped to be part of ENDURANCE's inaugural launch, she has had to shelve watching the bot in action for a future expedition.

Eventually the crew arrived at Lake Bonney, where they hoped to get the Bot House set up quickly. But as so many other Antarctic explorers have discovered, in Antarctica you should always be ready for the unexpected. As it had during the trial setup, the wind began gusting, even more strongly than at McMurdo. After eight hours, the Bot House was still not up. Exhausted from fighting the wind, the team finally repacked everything and waited for the next day, when setup went smoothly and ENDURANCE's support equipment, was installed. Assembling the bot inside the Bot House took another day.

Team members struggle with Antarctica's famous winds as they set up the Bot House on West Lake Bonney. The walls and the roof of the house are made from a large tarp stretched over seventeen arches made of pipe.

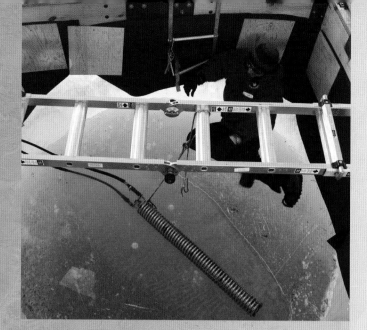

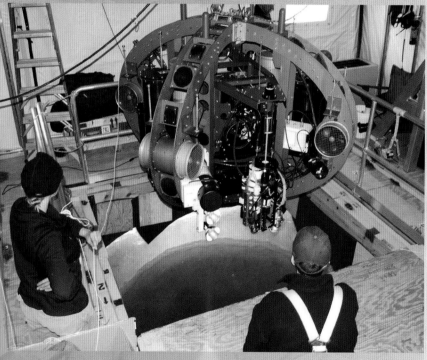

Top: An ENDURANCE team member checks the heating coil as it slowly melts a hole in the ice large enough for the bot to pass through. *Above:* Inside the Bot House, team members move ENDURANCE into place before final assembly.

THE BOT GOES EXPLORING

ENDURANCE performed well in its pre-Antarctica tests, but would the bot be able to withstand the rigors of Antarctica? Would its scientific equipment work? Before beginning its actual scientific measurements, the team put the bot through some field tests. It was good that they did.

To get the bot into the water, Doran's team first needed to melt a bot-sized hole. They drilled a 10-inch (25 cm) hole through the ice and suspended a melter, a power-operated heating coil, inside it. It took the melter almost two days, heating continuously, to create an 8-foot (2.5 m) melt hole for the bot. ENDURANCE slipped into the water without a glitch. Before lowering the bot into the water, Doran had dived into the melt hole and smoothed out any rough spots with an ice chipper. Other team members perfectly balanced the bot with weights so it would float in a level position. Everything looked great.

Of course, that's when the first surprise cropped up. When the team tried to lower the sonde, the equipment that unwinds the fiber-optic network cable wasn't working properly. The cable wouldn't unwind. If the cable does not unwind, the sonde cannot move up or down to take measurements at various depths—an essential part of its mission. Investigation revealed that even though the piece of equipment was designed to work in temperatures as cold as 32°F (0°C), it wouldn't work in Lake Bonney anytime the water temperature was less than 50°F (10°C), which it was. The problem turned out to be a temperature sensor that had been improperly set at the manufacturer. Bart Hogan, one of the team's engineers, did some rewiring that tricked the sensor into believing that the water temperature was warmer than it actually was. And voilà, ENDURANCE was back in fully operational condition.

Another surprise came when some of the bot's sensors suddenly stopped working. When the team raised the bot, they were perplexed by the bot's appearance: it was covered with fuzz! Closer examination revealed that the hairy-looking fuzz was actually thousands and thousands of minute air bubbles. Where had they all come from?

Lake Bonney's water is supersaturated with dissolved gases. *Supersaturated* means the water contains more of a dissolved substance than normally possible. Think about dissolving sugar in water. Eventually, you reach a point where the water won't dissolve any more sugar. That's a saturated solution. You can supersaturate the solution—force the water to dissolve and hold even more sugar than it normally can—by changing the normal conditions. For example, you can heat the water. When you do so, the sugar water solution becomes supersaturated. But a supersaturated solution is not very stable. If an object—called a "seed"—is put into the supersaturated solution, the dissolved material can separate out of the solution and settle around the seed. In Lake Bonney, the dissolved materials are gases. When ENDURANCE entered the water, it acted as the "seed." The gases separated from the water, forming air bubbles on the bot and covering the sensors. In this case, the solution—no pun intended—was simple: the team wiped the sensors with an environmentally friendly hand cleaner that prevented air bubbles from sticking to the sensors. One more bubbly issue remained. A bubble-coated bot is more buoyant than the bot normally is. Overcoming buoyancy to navigate into deeper water uses even more battery power than planned for. To correct this, the team added more weights to the bot, making it less buoyant.

The high concentration of dissolved gases in Lake Bonney caused an unexpected problem for researchers when those gases formed bubbles on the surface of ENDURANCE.

The ENDURANCE team. From left to right: Bill Stone, Chris Flesher, Vickie Siegel, Anika Taylor, Bart Hogan, Kristof Richmond, Shilpa Gulati, John Priscu, Peter Doran (in back, standing), Bob Kenworthy, and Maciej Obryk.

Having resolved the test-run problems, ENDURANCE was ready to tackle its scientific missions. The team had decided they would explore the western lobe of the lake. They set up an imaginary grid across the lake's surface, using the melt hole as the fixed point of reference. The scientists used GPS to determine the melt hole's exact location. The imaginary grid across the surface of the lake was like the lines that form the grid on a piece of graph paper. The squares of West Lake Bonney's grid measured 328 feet by 328 feet (100 m by 100 m). ENDURANCE traveled along a preprogrammed path up one grid line until it reached the final point in that line. Then it turned and looped back along the next parallel line. By doing this over a series of missions, the bot would eventually pass through all four corners of each box on the grid. Each of the corners, then, became a measured point. GPS allows the exact location of each point to be precisely plotted on a map.

On its quest for scientific measurements, the bot traveled away from the melt hole about 1 yard (1 m) below the ice ceiling at a speed of about 1 yard per second. When the bot reached each point on the grid, the thrusters that propel the bot through the water turned off. That's when the bot undertook an action that Peter Doran called "ice-picking." When the bot ice-picks, it floats upward until the four feet that stick up from the top of the bot rest against the ice. By ice-picking at each measuring point, the bot was stabilized so the sonde could collect its scientific data. At the same time, two team members walked along the ice surface and used a receiver to home in on magnetic pulses that were sent out from the bot. When they reached the spot directly above the bot, they marked the location with a brightly colored flag. GPS records the flag's location, and the record is used to compare and confirm the location that the bot's navigation system had recorded. It's a smart way to double-check that all systems are working properly.

At each of the grid's measuring points, the sonde was lowered through the water column until it was about 1 yard (1 m) from the bottom of the lake. There, the bot's camera took a picture of the lake bottom. Sensors inside the sonde measured the water properties at that depth. An instrument measured distances on the lake floor. This information would help the team create a 3-D map of the lake. Another instrument measured the temperature.

Connected to its base in the Bot House only by its 1,093-yard-long (1,000 m) fiber-optic tether cable, the bot ventured to the farthest reaches of West Lake Bonney. During the weeklong series of sampling runs, the bot had a few small problems. Once the cable snagged on an object that hung down from the ice ceiling. Another time the bot's buoyancy had to be readjusted to compensate for temperature changes in the water. (Very cold water pushes floating objects upward more strongly than warm water does.) And the team had some very tense moments when the bot lost its way. One of its navigation sensors stopped working after it bumped against an underwater ice ledge on the face of Taylor Glacier. Although its tether was still connected, the team sweated through several tense moments until they relocated the bot's exact location.

Each time a problem cropped up, the team solved it, and ENDURANCE safely made its way "home" using a special homing device that recognized and zeroed in on a blinking light pattern at the melt hole.

In the event that one of these encounters had disabled the bot at some distance from the melt hole, the team had a procedure in place for emergency recovery. Leaving a damaged bot in the lake would have been environmentally irresponsible. It was simply not an option.

Above: The bottom of Lake Bonney as seen by ENDURANCE. The red substance is probably iron seeping up from beneath the lake bottom. *Left:* Another ENDURANCE view of the bottom, this time showing the microbial mats that cover parts of the lake bottom.

SCUBA Dooba Doo!

In 2007 eight students at Rye Junior High, in New Hampshire, began their eighth-grade school year just like all the other students. At that time, they had no idea that at the end of the school year, they would willingly spend their summer vacation doing more schoolwork. As students in Robin Ellwood's science class, they volunteered for a fascinating project: to build a remotely operated vehicle that would be shipped to Antarctica for the 2008–2009 field season. There, the robot would dive in one of Antarctica's surface lakes, maybe even in Lake Bonney. And when it did, it would send pictures back to Rye Junior High via the Internet.

The students who built the bot, which they named SCUBADooba Doo, had little or no experience in science exploration—and they'd certainly never built a robot. "I had never imagined that I would take part in such a mechanical/engineering type project, since generally I am more interested in language arts than science," explained Maddie Cole, one of the student volunteers. But build a robot they did, and they learned a lot of new skills in the process.

SCUBADooba Doo's frame is made of PVC pipes, the kind plumbers often use for water pipes in houses. The students measured, cut, and glued the PVC themselves. After they built the frame, the student team added three motorized propellers to move the robot right, left, and up and down. The team also attached lights, a camera, and a 100-foot (30 m) tether cable, through which they controlled the robot and received photo images. To accomplish these tasks, the students learned how to strip and solder wires needed for electrical connections. Once all these connections were made, the robot had to be waterproofed as well.

SCUBADooba Doo's path to success, however, wasn't smooth. "What I remember most about building the robot was all the bumps in the road. We never really had a period of completely smooth sailing," said Maddie. "For instance, some of the materials listed in the instruction booklet didn't match with the supplies we were sent. We had an issue with the live-feed video camera because we connected some wires incorrectly. We mislabeled LEFT and RIGHT backward on our control box, which caused further complications." The challenges continued even after they'd assembled the robot. "After testing

Maddie Cole demonstrates some of SCUBADooba Doo's remote control features.

it in the pool of a local dive shop, we realized that the small foam blocks we had used to keep the tether afloat were flaking apart and disintegrating," Maddie recalled. This problem—a real environmental hazard to Antarctica—had to be solved. If it wasn't, SCUBADooba Doo would not be permitted to dive in Antarctica. Would the team be able to solve this major stumbling block? You bet! Foam noodles, the long strips people play with in swimming pools, proved to be the perfect solution. The team wrapped the frame and the tether with pieces of foam noodles. During later test dives in a saltwater pool, SCUBA's control box successfully maneuvered it through the water and the camera sent video clips back to the surface. On September 6, 2008, SCUBADooba Doo was packed into a rigid plastic case and sent to a cargo ship for its voyage to Antarctica.

After a successful test dive in a pool *(below, top)*, SCUBADooba Doo eventually proved itself in Antarctica when it explored the waters of McMurdo Sound *(below)*.

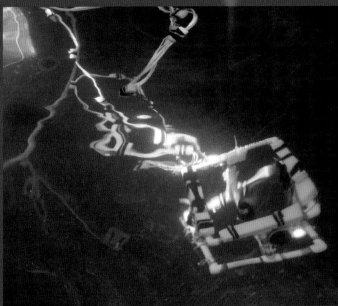

Although SCUBADooba Doo arrived safely, some disappointing news loomed on the robot's horizon. As Robin Ellwood explained, "We were hoping to send SCUBADooba Doo into the lakes. Unfortunately, due to a communication glitch, we were unable to acquire permission from the environmental people to launch it in the lakes. Since that wasn't able to happen, we were granted permission to launch it in McMurdo Sound."

On November 14, 2008, SCUBADooba Doo was launched into the frigid water of McMurdo Sound, where it performed—SUCCESSFULLY! It steered perfectly, its lights worked, and it sent great video clips to the surface where the scuba divers were swimming around it. SCUBA'S dive went global when a clip of its videos was posted on the Internet. "When I watched SCUBA on the Internet, it was a whole different experience for me," Maddie said. "Seeing SCUBA in action and knowing that it was able to be seen by people all over the world gave me a definite feeling of accomplishment. With such an amateur design crew, and keeping in mind all the problems we had had with SCUBA along the way, I guess I almost expected something to go wrong. And that made it all the better, when it did exactly what it was supposed to do and was being praised by the other scientists," Maddie added proudly.

SCUBADooba Doo's adventure has captured the attention and the imagination of other students at Rye Junior High. Plans are under way for a new, improved version of the bot. That means another science adventure is sure to follow.

ENDURANCE successfully carried out its mission in West Lake Bonney. It sampled the lake's water at 70 grid points. It took photos of the lake bottom and of the mats of microbial life-forms that cover parts of the lake floor. Data from the instruments proved that the bot could provide scientists with the information they needed to create maps of the lake bottom and the glacier face. It supplied the scientists with information about the chemical elements in the water and the kinds of life-forms that thrive under conditions that might resemble those on other planets. ENDURANCE proved to be a helpful tool for exploring extreme, remote underwater environments. In the coming months, the team will analyze all the data collected. Peter Doran and his colleagues feel certain that it will help solve some of Antarctica's surface lake secrets. And maybe someday, one of ENDURANCE's "great-grandkids" will be in outer space, sending back information from beneath Europa's ice-covered ocean.

STILL WATERS RUN DEEP

Surface lakes are only one of Antarctica's watery secrets. Geologists are also examining unexpected liquid water deep inside the continent's ice sheets.

In the 1960s, aircraft flyovers of Russia's Vostok Station, located far inland on the East Antarctic Ice Sheet, revealed an area of the ice sheet not far from the station that appeared smoother than the surrounding ice. Scientists wondered why. They theorized that if the ice sheet in that spot were lying on top of water, it might make the ice surface look smooth. But they had no way to prove this. And of course, the idea of water inside the ice seemed unusual.

Later, during the 1970s, scientists from Great Britain, the United States, and Denmark flew over the same area in aircraft equipped with ice-penetrating radar. They were gathering data about the mass of the ice sheet. As the scientists interpreted the patterns of radar waves, they noticed a peculiar change. Something deep beneath the ice sheet surface was reflecting the waves in an unexpected way. It wasn't the bedrock because the pattern was flat and smooth, and the pattern came from a depth much shallower than where the bottom of the ice sheet touched the bedrock. More radar data confirmed that these readings were accurate, as did examination of the area with seismic waves. Solving the mystery of the strange pattern hinged on knowing that radar waves and certain kinds of seismic waves do not travel through liquid water. When these waves reach liquid, they stop. Scientists had more good reason—and some proof—to believe there was liquid water under the ice.

In recent years, scientists have gathered more detailed information about the area with the use of another type of instrument, called a laser altimeter. An altimeter measures small changes in elevation of the surfaces of mountains, oceans, and ice sheets. Laser altimeters can be mounted on a plane or on a satellite orbiting Earth, and they take measurements by directing a short pulse of infrared light to the ice surface. The pulses bounce back to the altimeter much like the waves produced by ice-penetrating radar, except laser altimetry provides more precise measurements for the elevation of the ice surface and how it changes over a widespread area. In the area of the suspected water, it allowed scientists to create a well-defined, three-dimensional map of the smooth ice surface. Together, the information from ice-penetrating radar, seismic wave studies, and laser altimetry led scientists to an amazing conclusion: a very large lake exists deep within the ice sheet!

Lake Vostok station, home to the research teams that are uncovering the secrets of Lake Vostok

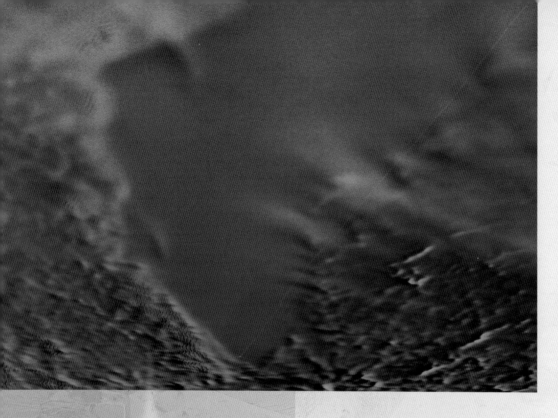

A satellite photo shows a smooth ice surface, a telltale sign of a lake hidden beneath the surface—Lake Vostok, in this case.

Because the lake lies beneath Vostok Station, geologists named it Lake Vostok. Scientists often compare the size of Lake Vostok to that of Lake Ontario, one of the Great Lakes in North America. However, Lake Vostok is much deeper. At its deepest points, Lake Vostok may be 3,000 feet (1,000 m) deep, making it one of the deepest lakes in the world. Also unlike Lake Ontario, you'd be hard-pressed to skip a stone on the water of Lake Vostok because its surface lies buried under almost 3 miles (5 km) of ice! As impossible as it seems, Lake Vostok's water, cradled in a rocky basin, remains in its liquid state despite being surrounded by freezing-cold glacial ice. But how does water in such a place remain a liquid?

The answer begins deep within Earth, in its core and mantle, where temperatures reach a scorching 6,650°F (3,677°C). Heat generated inside Earth is called geothermal heat. Geothermal heat radiates through Earth, sometimes traveling toward the surface, where it heats bedrock—bedrock like Lake Vostok's basin. That's part of the reason why the water remains unfrozen.

Another factor is the thermal blanket-like effect of the thick East Antarctic Ice Sheet. It prevents the geothermal heat from escaping. The temperature in many places along the bottom of Antarctica's ice sheets is, in fact, warm enough to melt ice. Lake Vostok stays liquid in much the same way Antarctic scientists learn to stay warm in a snow shelter at Happy Camper School.

The third factor that keeps Lake Vostok's water in a liquid state is the pressure of the ice. Enormous pressure can force solid matter to become liquid. It can force ice to melt. The pressure at the base of an ice sheet is so high that it actually lowers the temperature at which ice melts. On Earth's surface, ice melts at about 32°F (0°C). But the kind of pressure created by the thick Antarctic ice sheets can cause ice to melt at 28°F (−2°C).

It turns out that Lake Vostok is not unique. Since 1994 scientists have identified more than 150 lakes concealed deep within Antarctica's ice sheets. Because these lakes form beneath a glacier, they are called subglacial lakes. The basins that contain subglacial lakes were created long before today's ice sheets. Some of the basins formed during ancient mountain-building processes. Others formed during previous ice ages when ancient glaciers scooped away rock material.

Subglacial lakes are not all isolated from one another. Some of them are connected. Water flows from one subglacial lake to another according to the slope of the ice and the topography of the bedrock. Even though the flow occurs deep beneath the ice, geologists, using satellite laser altimetry, can monitor the movement. That's because when subglacial water flows from one area of an ice sheet to another, the surface of the ice rises and falls. Satellite altimeters record these changes in ice surface elevation. By tracking the changes in elevation, scientists can "watch" the pattern of subglacial water as it flows. Understanding how subglacial water moves could lead to new theories about how the Antarctic ice sheets behave.

Subglacial lakes excite scientists for many reasons. The ice that covers these lakes floats in a way that leads scientists to think that subglacial lake water is freshwater. If subglacial lake water were salty, scientists would expect a slight elevation of the ice surface. Salt water is denser than freshwater, so ice floats higher on top of salt water. But the surface doesn't appear to be elevated above subglacial lakes. And since no sunlight can filter through the thick ice, the waters must be perpetually dark and the levels of nutrients that plants and animals need to support life are likely very low. Despite the conditions, microorganisms may be living in subglacial lakes. Russian scientists sampled the ice sheet about 427 feet (130 m)

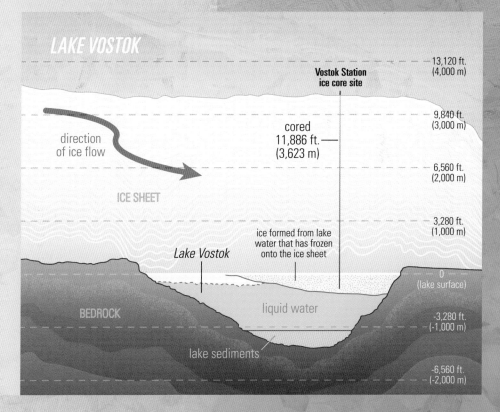

LAKE VOSTOK

Vostok Station
ice core site

direction
of ice flow

cored
11,886 ft.
(3,623 m)

ICE SHEET

ice formed from lake
water that has frozen
onto the ice sheet

Lake Vostok

liquid water

BEDROCK

lake sediments

13,120 ft.
(4,000 m)

9,840 ft.
(3,000 m)

6,560 ft.
(2,000 m)

3,280 ft.
(1,000 m)

0
(lake surface)

-3,280 ft.
(-1,000 m)

-6,560 ft.
(-2,000 m)

Organisms previously unknown to science might be found in Lake Vostok's mysterious waters. This scanning-electron micrograph shows an organism found in the ice just above Lake Vostok. Scientists are eager to study life-forms that can survive in such isolation.

above the surface of Lake Vostok and found cells of microorganisms that they believe may have been alive fairly recently. If microorganisms do exist in subglacial lakes, they have not had contact with other life-forms for hundreds of thousands, if not millions, of years. Organisms living under such extreme environmental conditions may have adapted in a very different manner from their counterparts that live on or near Earth's surface. If this is true, it is possible that unique life-forms may live in Antarctica's subglacial lakes.

Scientists are as excited by what might *not* be in the lakes as they are by what is. Sealed as they are from the rest of Earth, subglacial lakes offer a chance to look at pristine environments that are unchanged and uncontaminated since the ice formed long ago. The lakes are a kind of time capsule. Thick ice caps prevent modern pollution from entering the water. This is a unique situation. Even the Pacific Ocean's Mariana Trench, which is the deepest place in the world's oceans, is likely to contain some contaminants. Unless humans inadvertently introduce them (for example, during water sampling procedures), modern contaminants have no way to enter the closed system of a subglacial lake.

A multinational team of scientists, led by researchers from Great Britain, are busy exploring Lake Ellsworth, a small subglacial lake in the West Antarctic Ice Sheet, with the goal of learning more about the geology of these lakes. Located at the base of the Ellsworth Mountains, the lake is covered by ice that is 2 miles (3 km) thick. The lake's basin is actually an old fjord, or deep valley, carved out of the seafloor by a glacier that existed before the present West Antarctic Ice Sheet. Because the lake is small and the region much more accessible than areas on the East Antarctic Ice Sheet, the team is confident their exploration will shed new light on one of Antarctica's fascinating features.

One thing the scientists already know is that the story of the water that fills Lake Ellsworth is one of ancient precipitation. Scientists can learn about ancient Earth from this old water. Martin Siegert is a glaciologist, a geologist who specializes in studying glaciers. According to Siegert, "Glacial ice that melts into the lake was deposited as snow upstream of the lake more than a hundred thousand years ago." In a process that took thousands of years, that snow was buried by new layers of snow and was compressed until it became glacial ice. And then, as it lay deeply buried, geothermal heat began melting the ice. The water pooled in the basin and created Lake Ellsworth.

A field camp on Lake Ellsworth. Vinson Massif, the highest mountain on the continent, looms in the background.

British scientists on Lake Ellsworth use a small explosion to create a seismic wave that will help them measure the depth of the lake.

If all goes according to plan, the Lake Ellsworth project scientists will drill into the lake during the 2012–2013 field season and sample the water and the sediments. The researchers are committed to investigating the lake using ultraclean equipment and sampling techniques that will not adversely affect the lake's environment. They will do this by using a hot-water drill to bore down through the ice sheet and into the lake. The hot water will come from melting snow and ice from the area around the drill hole and will be filtered to remove any particles it may contain. In this stage of the program, after the drill reaches the lake, a probe will be lowered into the water to test it for life-forms. The group also plans to remove a core of sediment from the lake floor. These sediments likely hold important clues about Earth's past climates. From the information collected, the scientists may be able to predict future climate changes and their effects—for example, a rise or fall in Earth's sea level.

As Siegert and his colleagues continue to explore Lake Ellsworth, they hope to be able to determine the age of the lake. "It could be as young as 1.5 to 2 million years old, or it could be 15 million years old. This is one of the big questions for us to answer," Siegert said. The answer to that question may also help them determine the age of the West Antarctic Ice Sheet, a fact that will help scientists better predict how the sheet might change in the future.

They also hope that examining the lake's microbial life will help us understand more about how life develops in a sunless environment. Might we learn how an organism sustains life by using chemicals, like those found in the lake's water and sediments, for survival rather than sunlight? Could we discover more information about how life adapts to living under tremendous pressure, like that of a heavy ice sheet? Siegert and his colleagues eagerly anticipate the opportunity to explore one of Earth's final frontiers.

For as long as people have walked on Earth's surface, that "frontier" has rested solidly on top of the South Pole. But it hasn't always been snow-covered nor has it always been near the South Pole. In fact, Antarctica's story began millions of years ago, in a place far from the bottom of the world, in a time when Earth's continents were very different from the continents we see today.

CHAPTER 4

Once Upon a Time

IF YOU SUDDENLY FOUND YOURSELF STANDING IN A LUSH GREEN FOREST, CHEST DEEP IN FERNS, WITH SWEAT BEADING ON YOUR BROW, "I'M IN ANTARCTICA!" MIGHT NOT BE THE FIRST THOUGHT THAT COMES TO MIND. If you lived millions of years ago, though, it just might be. And it probably wouldn't be long before you would discover that other large animals were also in the area.

Geologists read Earth's history in its rock, and the most startling revelation of that history is how much the face of the planet has changed over 4.5 billion years, the age of the oldest known rocks on Earth. As recently as 250 million years ago, Earth had one continent, not seven. Geologists call this supercontinent Pangaea, a Greek word meaning "all lands" or "all earth." As Pangaea broke apart and new continents formed and separated, conditions for life on Earth changed drastically, and scientists can see the evidence of those changes in the fossils found on Antarctica.

This computer rendering shows Earth at the time Pangaea began breaking up, around two hundred million years ago.

FOSSILS FROM THE JOURNEY SOUTH

Today, whales and seals cruise in the water along the Antarctic coast. Birds such as skuas and petrels soar in the sky, and penguins waddle on the rocky shore. But the only plants those penguins will encounter onshore are two kinds of flowering plants and some mosses and lichens. There are no trees. No shrubs. The terrain becomes even more desolate farther inland. Eventually, there is nothing but ice and rock. There are no living creatures at all. Yet the land was not piled high with thick ice at the time it pulled away from Pangaea and began its long, slow journey to the South Pole. At times during those long-ago years, its climate was hot and steamy and the land flourished with lush forests. Other times, it was more moderate. At one time or another, all of Antarctica teemed with plants and animals. Those life-forms are still frozen there, but not in ice. Instead, Antarctica's ancient life is frozen in stone in the form of fossils.

Scientists have collected fossils on Antarctica since the earliest days of the continent's exploration. Robert Falcon Scott recognized that fossils contained important information about Antarctica's history. About 35 pounds (16 kilograms) of rocks, many containing fossils, were found among the remains of his ill-fated voyage to the South Pole. The plant fossils that Scott's expedition collected were among the first found in Antarctica. Since then, paleontologists have collected many thousands of pounds of rocks that contain plant and animal fossils.

These fossils supply evidence that 240 million years ago, life thrived throughout the area we call Antarctica. Certain of those plants and animal fossils also confirm that Antarctica was once a part of the abundantly alive continent of Gondwanaland, a continent created when Pangaea split apart about 200 million years ago. One fossil souvenir of Gondwanaland is of a large plant called *Glossopteris*. *Glossopteris* is now extinct, but its fossils remain as souvenirs and proof of a long-lost continent.

Edith Taylor has been collecting plant fossils in Antarctica for many years. She is a paleobotanist, a scientist who studies ancient plant life. When she studies *Glossopteris* trunks, she looks for a pattern of thin circular rings, just like the rings you can see on any tree stump. These are growth rings. Growth rings are made of plant cells and are added annually as a tree or large shrub grows. If frost damages the tree's growth, it creates a frost ring, or a layer of plant cells that appear damaged due to freezing. Taylor has not found frost rings in the Antarctic *Glossopteris* fossils that she has examined.

Top: Fossils of *Glossopteris* leaves have been found in many areas that were once part of Gondwanaland. *Left:* An artist's rendering shows a *Glossopteris* tree and its leaves which could grow to lengths over 12 inches (30 cm) long.

Her findings indicate that the climate was mild during the seasons when the plants grew—certainly not the year-round deep freeze that we associate with the modern continent.

So *Glossopteris* fossils tell scientists that Antarctica was warmer once, but how does a fossilized piece of a tree help prove Antarctica was part of Gondwanaland? *Glossopteris* fossils are not found only in Antarctica. They have also been found in Africa, South America, India, and Australia, places widely separated from one another. The seeds of *Glossopteris* were too large and heavy to be carried by wind across the long ocean distances between these continents. So how did the seeds get dispersed? Scientists conclude that *Glossopteris* forests came to be so widespread because these lands were joined together as part of a larger continent for millions of years. Flying creatures, walking animals, and running water most likely carried the large seeds from one place to another throughout the huge landmass.

At the same time that *Glossopteris* flourished on Antarctica, an animal called *Lystrosaurus* walked the land. This chunky, short-tailed creature was about the size of a pig. It looked like a lizard, but its four legs were positioned more vertically under its body, like a pig's, rather than the sprawling legs of a crocodile that keep the reptile close to the ground.

An artist's rendering of *Lystrosaurus*

Since *Lystrosaurus* was an herbivore, it's possible it may have been one of the animals that carried *Glossopteris* seeds to new places. Like *Glossopteris*, fossils of *Lystrosaurus* are widespread and have been found in Australia, Antarctica, India, and Africa, providing additional proof that all of these places were part of Gondwanaland.

Fossils show that over millions of years, life on the land that became Antarctica evolved, creating new species of plants and animals. Antarctica has been home to trees and ferns. Fossils of ancient species of fish and amphibians show that parts of Antarctica's mainland were once underwater. Insects, reptiles, and mammals flew, crawled, and ran across the land. But perhaps the most startling life-form to call Antarctica home is a group of reptiles called thecodonts, which gradually evolved into dinosaurs.

Members of William Hammer's team look down from their dig site, 13,000 feet (4,000 m) above sea level. This site is one of the most challenging paleontological sites on Earth.

ANTARCTIC DINOSAURS

Like so many other scientific tasks, collecting fossils on the Antarctic mainland is a challenge. Dinosaur fossils have been found on Seymour Island, Vega Island, and James Ross Island, all located off the coast of the Antarctic Peninsula. But the rock outcrops on these islands, where dinosaur fossils are found, are almost completely ice-free in the summer. Reaching the outcrops and excavating the fossils is fairly easy. That's not the case where paleontologist William Hammer and his colleagues work. Hammer's team works far inland, high atop Mount Kirkpatrick, in the Transantarctic Mountains. The outcrops where they collect fossils are about 13,000 feet (4,000 m) above sea level—high enough that a person will notice the lack of oxygen. Hammer and his team

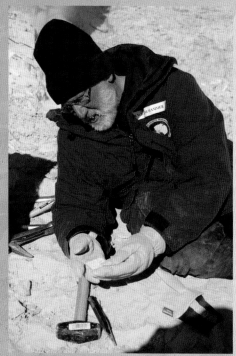

Right: William Hammer unearthing a fossil using rock hammers. *Below:* Sometimes more drastic measures are required. Hammer's team also used jackhammers to free large blocks of rock containing the fossils.

can only work on Mount Kirkpatrick in the summer. Even then, at that altitude, the temperature only reaches –25°F (–32°C) during the day.

Conditions on Mount Kirkpatrick make it impossible to camp near the rock outcrop that contains the fossils they study. So each day a helicopter flies them up the mountain, a distance of about 40 miles (64 km) from their base camp. At times, however, the wind conditions are too dangerous for the helicopter to attempt the flight. Those days, the crew works in camp.

"Sometimes we have wrapping and crating of fossils to work on, but if it is too windy to fly, it is generally too windy to work outside," Hammer stated. When the team must remain inside their tents, they keep themselves occupied by reading or working on a laptop in the communications hut.

William Hammer has spent many seasons fossil hunting in the Transantarctic Mountains. But one of his most exciting finds occurred late in 1990. It began when David Elliot, a geologist who was also working on Mount Kirkpatrick, stumbled across something he hadn't expected: fossil bones! From the size and shape of the bones he saw, Elliot knew that they had belonged to a large vertebrate. He also knew that the rock that contained the bones was about 200 million years old.

Elliot radioed Hammer, who was working on a fossil site farther down the mountain. Knowing how rare it is to find the fossil remains of large vertebrates in Antarctica, Hammer was eager to check out Elliot's find. As soon as he saw the bones embedded in the rock, Hammer knew he was looking at the skeleton of a dinosaur—the first dinosaur bones ever found on mainland Antarctica!

These tantalizing glimpses weren't enough for Hammer to identify the bones with any certainty. So, for the time being, the kind of dinosaur Elliot had discovered remained a mystery. Hammer and his crew spent the rest of that field season using a jackhammer to remove large sections of fossil-filled rock from the outcrop. Smaller sections were removed with rock hammers. While this type of work is "business as usual" for most geologists, working at a site where fierce winds blow at a moment's notice and temperatures plummet without warning is not.

Hammer acknowledged that while his crew is up at the site, they are always prepared for the unexpected. "If the helicopter can't get up to the site to pick us up, we have survival bags to break into. We have one survival bag for every two people. Each bag includes a small tent, two sleeping bags, a camp stove with fuel, some freeze-dried food packets, and a few comic books for amusement." Struggling against windy, raw conditions, the paleontologists removed 5,000 pounds (2,268 kg) of fossil-filled rocks, which were transported by helicopter to the crew's base camp.

As chunks of rock arrived in base camp, Hammer examined the fossils, but the bones were still surrounded by too much rock for identification. The more Hammer looked, however, the more he began to suspect that the rocks contained the remains of more than one animal. But he couldn't be sure.

Base Camp

Hammer's facilities at his base camp weren't exactly ideal for conclusive study of the rock. "We use Scott tents, which are like big pyramids. They're made of real heavy canvas and big poles, which makes them sturdy in the wind," Hammer explained.

As you might have guessed, Scott tents *(shown below)* are named for Robert Falcon Scott. To this day, scientists do their work in a tent designed over a century ago. Of course, the environment in tents is warmer than the powerful, flesh-numbing winds that blow downhill off the mountains. Even so, it still gets pretty cold inside the tents, and ice buildup on the inside surface of the tent can be a problem. "The moisture from your breath freezes on the canvas and it builds up on the inside of the tent. It can form a sheet of ice," Hammer said. To protect themselves from falling ice, the scientists put netting on the inner surface of the tent. "The netting causes the moisture to freeze on the strings and it falls off in little pieces rather than forming a big sheet," said Hammer.

Ultimately, thorough study of the fossils would require a laboratory facility away from Antarctica. So the crew carefully packed the fossil-filled rocks into crates. At the end of the field season, the crates were flown to Ross Island and then shipped by boat to the United States. Several months later, they arrived in Hammer's laboratory in Rock Island, Illinois, at 700 feet (213 m) above sea level and where the temperature was around 68°F (20°C)—quite a change from their previous home!

Using an electric tool called an air scribe, which is like a tiny jackhammer, the paleontologists painstakingly freed the fossilized bones from their stone coffins. Even in a warm laboratory far away from Antarctica, this was slow work. It took almost a year to completely expose the dinosaur's skull, which was almost 2 feet (0.6 m) long. Standing beneath the re-assembled skeleton (made with casts of the actual bones), three words come to mind: Teeth. Talons. Sharp. This was definitely a meat eater! The dinosaur was about 22 feet (6.7 m) long, and it walked upright on two legs, like the dinosaur called *Tyrannosaurus rex*. After examining all the bones, Hammer realized that his crew had found a species of dinosaur that no one had ever found before.

The first scientist to describe a new species in a scientific journal gets to choose the organism's scientific name. Hammer named the dinosaur *Cryolophosaurus ellioti*. The first part of the name, *Cryolophosaurus*, means "frozen crested lizard," so named for a bony ridge called a crest that stuck up from the top of the skull. The second part, *ellioti*, comes from David Elliot's last name. Elliot was the scientist who had first spotted the bones.

Hammer's suspicion that the rocks contained the fossils of more than one animal was correct. His team also found a wing bone from a flying reptile called a pterosaur and teeth that belonged to at least two other dinosaur species. Since some of the *Cryolophosaurus's* bones

Lab technician ReBecca Hunt Foster works with an air scribe to free delicate fossilized *Cryolophosaurus* vertebrae from the surrounding rock.

had tooth marks on them, Hammer thinks the teeth belonged to dinosaurs that ate *Cryolophosaurus*'s flesh after it died.

Paleontologists don't often figure out exactly why an ancient animal died, but for this particular dinosaur, Hammer believes he knows. While one of Hammer's team was using the air scribe to clean the skull, he found two rib bones of a plant-eating dinosaur inside the jaws of the *Cryolophosaurus*. Hammer thinks the bones may have belonged to a *Glacialisaurus*. Hammer is sure that *Cryolophosaurus* choked to death while eating.

Above: *Cryolophosaurus*'s skeleton
Left: This artist's rendering shows how *Cryolophosaurus* might have looked.

The discoveries made by Hammer's crew reveal an Antarctica that looked very different from its current barren, icy landscape. The rocks that contained *Cryolophosaurus* are made of mud that had petrified, or turned into stone. This kind of mud is found near rivers. The crew also found fossils of trees that do not grow in cold places. Taken together, the presence of reptiles, flowing water, and plants clearly show that the land that would become Antarctica was a much warmer place 200 million years ago.

Fossils found in other places on the continent reveal that the climate was still warm millions of years after *Cryolophosaurus* had become extinct. In 2005 a team of U.S. and Argentinean paleontologists found the fossil remains of a 5-foot-long (1.5 m) juvenile plesiosaur on Vega Island. Plesiosaurs were marine reptiles that lived about 70 million years ago. These creatures, which could grow as long as 32 feet (10 m), had long necks, a tail, and four paddle-shaped fins that they used for swimming. The well-preserved remains of the young plesiosaur were only missing the skull, which had been worn away by wind and ice. Partial remains from two other plesiosaurs and some shorebirds were found near the fossilized bones. All the remains lay buried beneath a layer of volcanic ash. This led the team to conclude that the animals died during a volcanic eruption. The rock formation that contains the fossils is about 650 feet (198 m) above sea level. Since plesiosaurs live in the ocean, 70 million years ago that land must have been under the sea. Mountain-building forces inside Earth later raised the land.

As time passed, the animals that lived in the area that would become Antarctica changed. Dinosaurs became extinct. About 45 million years ago, Antarctica and Australia, which had been joined together, began to drift apart. The Antarctic climate was still hospitable for animal and plant life though. Again, fossil remains prove this. In fact, 40 million years ago, a hoofed mammal about the size of a small horse roamed the area that became Seymour Island. Separated in time by 30 million years from the young plesiosaur, the hoofed mammal shows that water had receded from that region of Antarctica. The land had changed from a habitat suitable to a swimming reptile to one suitable for a plant-eating, land-dwelling mammal.

FREEZE-DRIED SURPRISES

Not every Antarctic fossil is as dramatic as a dinosaur. And it doesn't take tons of rock for scientists to get a peek into Antarctica's past. The tiny debris left behind by glaciers contain many fascinating secrets. By observing and analyzing glacial deposits in Antarctica, scientists hope to answer a couple of burning questions: When did Antarctica's climate become frigid? When did the West and East Antarctic ice sheets begin to consume the continent?

Allan Ashworth, Adam Lewis, and David Marchant are members of a team of glacial geologists and paleontologists. They think they may have found the answers. The trail of evidence began in November 2000 with the discovery of many thin layers of papery brown and white materials in a small basin that had once been a lake. Located in the Olympus

The Olympus Range as seen from the Dry Valleys

This moss fossil is evidence that Antarctica's climate was warmer in the past.

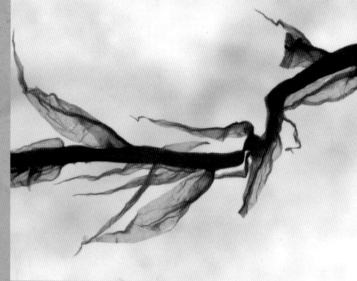

Using a microscope, Ashworth's team was able to examine the delicate structure of a piece of the freeze-dried moss.

Range in the Dry Valleys, the lake had developed in a way similar to other ancient lake beds in the area. As an ancient mountain glacier melted, it deposited rocks and sediment into a hill called a moraine. The moraine spanned the valley the glacier had occupied. As the glacier receded, the moraine blocked the glacial meltwater from flowing down the valley. Instead, the meltwater pooled in the basin created by the moraine and formed a lake. The lake drained thousands of years ago, but it left much behind for scientists to study.

A close look at the brown layered material revealed 1 inch-long (2.5 cm) shreds of a fibrous substance. The team wasn't sure what they'd found. They collected samples and brought them back to camp, where they could be examined with a microscope. Astonishingly, the shreds turned out to be the freeze-dried stems and leaves of a kind of moss that lived in shallow water—the kind of water found along the muddy edges of a lake. Even more amazing, when the team put some of the freeze-dried moss into water, the leaves and stems absorbed the water and the thin shreds plumped up and looked like plants again. This kind of moss no longer grows on mainland Antarctica. It's simply too cold. Similar modern mosses can only survive in places where the summer temperature averages 29°F (–1.7°C). The area's mean summer temperature in modern times is about 10°F (–12°C).

The brown layer of sediments also contained pollen, tiny grains that are found in the reproductive parts of plants. One of the pollen grains that the team found came from a group of trees called *Nothofagus*, also known as southern beech trees, because today they grow in South America, New Zealand, and Tasmania. Today, no trees or shrubs are in this area, but the presence of *Nothofagus* pollen proves that trees did exist in that area at one time. However, in the sediment from the lake they did not find any fossils of leaves or wood from these trees. That suggests that the trees did not grow precisely in the area of the lake, which was at a high elevation. But they grew close enough to the area that the pollen could be carried up into the lake by the wind. Both the mosses and the pollen help to establish the conditions of one of that area's past climates, one where the plants clung to life under conditions that just squeaked inside the climatic limits for their growth.

The layers containing the powdery white material were no less interesting. They consisted of the remains of diatoms. Diatoms are microscopic algae that live in freshwater or salt water. They also live on plant surfaces and in damp soils. Where there's water, there are likely to be diatoms. "Some live in shallow water, some live in deep water—they can even be found in tap water," explained Allan Ashworth.

Diatoms have only one cell, but they can connect with other diatoms to form small groups called colonies. The cell wall of a diatom is made of silica, which forms a glasslike shell around diatoms. Silica is a naturally made chemical compound that contains the elements silicon and oxygen. The silica shells of diatoms vary in shape according to species. About one hundred thousand species of diatoms exist, some of which live on Antarctica. When a diatom dies, the shell remains behind and can fossilize. Since diatoms live in many different environments and climates, the shapes of their fossilized shells can tell paleontologists much about conditions in the past.

In the lake bed in the Dry Valleys, the fossil diatoms helped the team to understand the ancient lake's varied history. "The discovery of the fossils turned out to be a real treasure trove of goodies. They provided more of the clues necessary to unlock the climate secrets of the continent," stated Ashworth. The various species of diatom fossils present in different layers indicated that sometimes the lake was shallow and other times it was as deep as 26 feet (8 m). However, none of the diatoms that they found in the ancient lake basin are

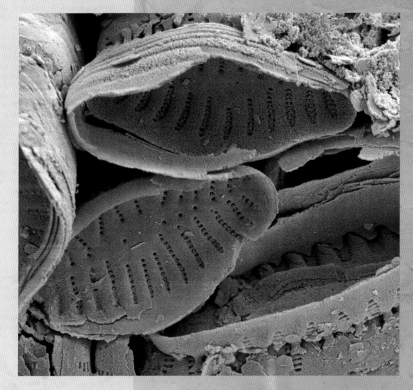

Diatoms like these offer scientists microscopic clues about past environments.

like the diatoms that exist in Antarctica now, which, once again, reinforced the conclusion that Antarctica has had very different climates.

The team also found fossils of another kind of tiny organism, a shrimplike creature called an ostracod. The pin-head-sized fossils found in the lake's sediment were a freshwater species and were extremely well-preserved. Like the freeze-dried mosses, the ostracods found in the lake's sediment can only survive where the average summer temperatures are about 34°F (1°C). No ostracods of this type live on Antarctica today.

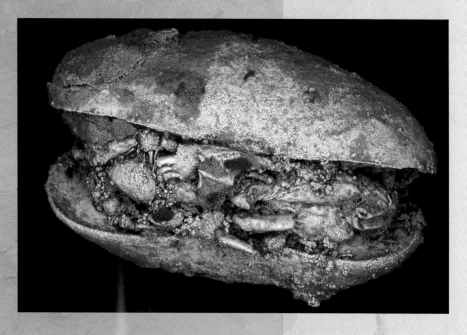

This ostracod lived at a time when freshwater surface lakes occupied the area now known as the Dry Valleys.

Other than the mosses, pollen, diatoms, and the remains of a beetle, the ancient lake doesn't appear to have been a habitat for other notable life-forms. By comparing the ancient lake's conditions to those of modern lakes that have similar conditions, the scientists determined that the area had been a lot like present-day northern Canada and Alaska.

But when did the conditions in this area change from the ancient warmer climate to today's permanently cold climate? Stratigraphy and an ancient volcanic eruption supplied the answer to this question. One of the principles of stratigraphy is that in a sequence of undisturbed sediment deposits, the bottom sediments were deposited first. A layer of volcanic ash that was 1.1 inches (3 cm) thick lay among the layers of sediments that contained the diatoms and the moss fossils. That meant the ash layer had been deposited after some of the sediments that contained the fossils, but before others. If the geologists could discover how old the ash was, they could determine the age of the lake sediments.

A chemical element in the ash called argon provided the information the geologists needed to solve this mystery. Sidney Hemming and Malka Machlus, two members of the team, used a scientific instrument called a mass spectrometer to detect and analyze the argon in the ash. Hemming and Machlus determined that the ash layer was about 14 million years old.

"At the ancient lake site today, the only forms of life that survive are bacteria that live in the soils and small lichens that live on the rocks. As cold and uninviting as the environment is now, it's hard to imagine a small lake with sunlight reflecting on the surface and beetles crawling through vegetation on the margins where today only barren rocky slopes exist," said Ashworth. "The change in climate from warmer and wetter to colder and drier at 14 million years ago caused the local extinction of the mosses, diatoms, ostracods, and beetles." The change appears to have occurred fairly rapidly, perhaps within thousands of years. While that seems like a long time, when compared to the age of Earth—4.5 billion years—it's almost like the blink of an eye.

The work of scientists like Hammer, Ashworth, Lewis, and Marchant provides a basic outline of the history of Antarctica's climate from millions of years ago to as recent as thousands of years ago. This is not just history for its own sake, though. Scientists of all specialties are contributing to a growing body of knowledge about Antarctica's past. Together, they increase the scientific community's ability to use the past to help them understand what may happen in Earth's near future. And Antarctica figures large in today's discussions about climate change.

Scientists Adam Lewis *(left)* and Allan Ashworth in the Dry Valleys

CHAPTER 5

The Antarctic Crystal Ball

ANTARCTICA IS THOUSANDS OF MILES AWAY FROM THE PLACES WHERE MOST OF US WORK, GO TO SCHOOL, AND LIVE. Out of sight should not be out of mind, though. Studying Antarctica's past and present conditions is helping scientists predict how Earth's climate may change in the future. And those changes will affect everyone.

For more than a century, scientists have known that Antarctica's isolation makes it one of Earth's best laboratories for the study of natural change. As Peter Doran and his colleagues gather data at Lake Bonney, they are adding new observations to a record that stretches back to Robert Falcon Scott's Antarctic expeditions. In his journal on June 26, 1911, Scott wrote the following lines about changes he and others had noticed at Lake Bonney:

Mention was made of the difference of water [level] found in Lake Bonney by me in December 1903 and the Western Party [the expedition members who were based at Camp Evans] in February 1911. It seems certain that water must go on accumulating in the lake during the two or three summer months, and it is hard to imagine that all can be lost again by the winter's evaporation. If it does, "evaporation" becomes a matter of primary importance.

The question of what causes change on Antarctica has long been a fascinating one.

SIFTING THROUGH THE GASEOUS CLUES

What have modern scientists learned so far from Antarctica's ancient history? A great deal and often from very small sources. For climatologists, scientists who specialize in studying climates and how they change, each tiny air bubble in an ice core is like opening a tiny window

Scientific measurements show that the temperatures in some areas of Antarctica have warmed during the years from 1957 to 2006. The rate of this fifty-year warming trend has been greater than 0.2°F (0.1°C) per decade. The rise in temperature is strongest in winter and spring. Red-colored areas show the warming trend, which is greatest on the Antarctic Peninsula and in West Antarctica.

into Earth's past. These bubbles contain samples of the gases that were present in Earth's atmosphere in that area when the bubble formed. When examining information gathered from ice cores, climatologists measure the level of many different gases, but the levels of two gases particularly interest them. The first is a colorless, odorless gas called carbon dioxide. Carbon dioxide is the gas that leaves your body when you exhale. It's also one of the gases that is produced when people burn fuels such as oil, coal, and natural gas.

Methane, the second gas that interests these scientists, is not odorless. It's the stinky gas often found in swamps, garbage dumps, and livestock farms. Methane—and its odor—is produced when bacteria and other microscopic organisms cause plant remains and animal wastes to decompose. Decomposing garbage, mining, oil and gas production, and the various ways people use and manage land produce about two-thirds of Earth's total methane gas. But what do the levels of carbon dioxide and methane in the atmosphere today have to do with Antarctica and its ice sheets?

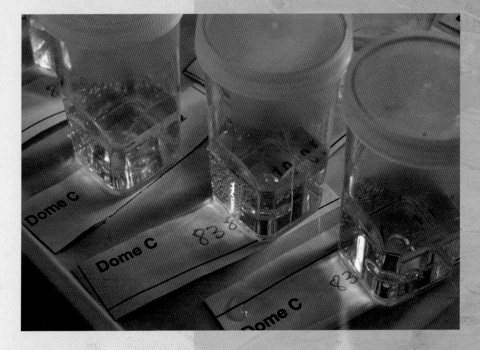

Samples of ice from Dome C cores await analysis, the results of which give scientists a look at ancient levels of carbon dioxide and methane.

These two gases are called greenhouse gases because they trap heat inside Earth's atmosphere, just like a greenhouse traps warm, moist air. While carbon dioxide is really good at trapping heat, methane is even better. Over a one-hundred-year period, methane can capture sixty times the amount of heat energy than carbon dioxide can! When Earth's atmosphere contains a lot of greenhouse gases, Earth's overall temperature rises. The increase in average temperature is what scientists mean when they use the term *global warming*. If Earth warms by an average of two or three degrees, the climates of some areas on Earth are likely to change.

The carbon dioxide and methane contained in the air bubbles found inside the ice core from Dome C, on the East Antarctic Ice Sheet, shows that atmospheric levels of both gases rose and fell, recording highs and lows eight times during the time period represented in the

Change before Our Eyes

Is there any easily seen evidence of a change in air temperature in Antarctica? In 1986, when geologist Reed Scherer saw the dog remains at Shackleton's 1915 supply depot at Camp Evans, he photographed one of them *(above)*. In 2006, Scherer revisited the remains and noticed something startling: the dog remains, perfectly preserved for almost one hundred years, are now rotting *(right)*. This is the result of warmer temperatures that permit the kinds of bacteria that cause decay to flourish. In other places, Antarctic grasses are growing in places farther inland than previously seen.

ice core. Each time the levels of the two gases rose and fell, the air temperature rose and fell along with them. The evidence indicates that in the past, when the levels of carbon dioxide and methane in the atmosphere rose, Earth's global climate got warmer. And when that happens, glaciers and ice sheets shrink.

Antarctica is both the repository for information about Earth's ancient climates and the early warning system for its present one. During ancient times, carbon dioxide has ranged from a low of about 180 parts per million (ppm) to as high as about 300 ppm. The size of the ice sheets responded to those levels, growing when carbon dioxide levels fell and shrinking when they rose. Since the early 1800s, the levels of carbon dioxide and methane gases in the atmosphere have skyrocketed. As of 2010, the carbon dioxide level in the atmosphere is about 385 ppm and rising. This sharp increase, most scientists believe, is due to human activity.

THAW?

Scientists predict that the carbon dioxide level in the atmosphere will continue to rise. Should this occur, how might Antarctica's ice sheets behave in the future? First, if air temperatures increase, ice would obviously melt faster, but when Antarctic ice melts, it's not like an ice cube melting into a puddle on a hot sidewalk. Melting Antarctic ice can be dramatic, even violent. The Larsen Ice Shelf, along the coast of the Antarctic Peninsula, was an ice shelf made of three sections, called Larsen A, B, and C. In January 1995, a large portion of the smallest section, Larsen A, disintegrated into icebergs during a storm. During the early 1990s, the peninsula experienced several warm summers in a row. At the time, scientists theorized that the unusual warm summers may have contributed to Larsen A's disintegration. At the end of January 2002, the 720-foot-thick (220 m) Larsen B rapidly began collapsing. In a little more than five weeks, this ice shelf section, which geologists believe had existed for more than four hundred years and maybe as many as twelve thousand years, had completely disintegrated into a field of icebergs. Scientists continue to monitor Larsen C, the largest section of the ice shelf, to see if it is remaining stable.

What happened to the Larsen Ice Shelf was not an isolated incident. In April 2009, a 270-square-mile (700 sq. km) section of the Wilkins Ice Shelf, located on the western Antarctic Peninsula, broke apart. The area of breakage was about the size of New York City.

The changes don't end there. The Amundsen Sea fringes the western coast of Antarctica. The Pine Island Ice Shelf extends into this sea. Two large glaciers, Pine Island Glacier and Thwaites Glacier, feed the Pine Island Ice Shelf. These two glaciers are so large that geologists estimate that about one-third of the ice contained in the West Antarctic Ice Sheet drains from them. Geologists have been monitoring the ice plain along the front of Pine Island Glacier. An ice plain is the area of an ice sheet that lies on the surface just before the sheet begins to float free of its land anchor. (Remember, when an ice sheet begins to float, that area becomes an ice shelf.) In 2004 scientists observed that the ice plain had gotten so thin that they became concerned that it might lose touch with the ground surface below. If that happened, the thinned ice could break up, perhaps like Larsen B and the Wilkins ice shelves.

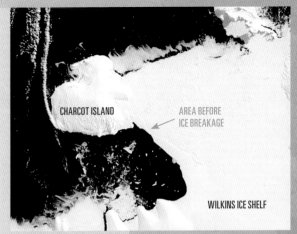

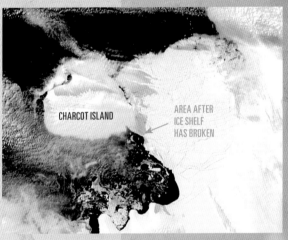

Before April 2009, ice bridged the area between Charcot Island and the Wilkins Ice Shelf *(top)*. By April 6, 2009, the ice bridge had collapsed, littering the sea with icebergs, including one the size of New York City. Water, appearing as a dark line along the right side of the island, now separates the ice and the ice shelf *(above)*.

Moreover, in recent years, Pine Island Glacier has been speeding up, carrying ice more rapidly toward the sea. For now, the ice plain and ice shelf act as a barrier between the glacier and the sea. If the ice plain thins, begins to float, and then breaks apart, the Pine Island Glacier would be able to flow rapidly to the sea. In an even more dramatic scenario, glaciers in other areas could feed into the sea if the whole West Antarctic Ice Sheet were to break up.

Just how big a cause for concern the changes at Pine Island Glacier are is the important question. Once again, this is where Antarctica's long record of historical climate data pays off. Climate models are computer-generated scenarios that predict how Earth's climate may change in the future. Models are made by using many types of historical data, including air and sea temperatures and the amount of greenhouse gases in the atmosphere. Climate models can create video simulations that show the formation of Antarctica's present ice sheets. These models indicate that over time the ice sheets exhibited a pattern of growing and shrinking. Each time they grew, they grew a bit larger until, finally, ice consumed the entire continent. Computer models also show that the breakup of large areas of ice—the West Antarctic Ice Sheet, for example—might occur in much the same fashion. It's normal for an ice shelf to lose ice due to seasonal melting and when ice calves off into the sea, becoming an iceberg. But this loss is normally replaced as new ice is added to the ice shelf from land-based glaciers. In this scenario, the overall size of the ice shelf is maintained. If, however, the average

Aerial photography and other measurements from planes are among the ways scientists study change in the Pine Island Glacier and its ice shelf. The photo below shows the calving front of the Pine Island Ice Shelf, where ice breaks from the ice shelf and splashes into the sea.

temperature of the air and of the sea increases by even a couple of degrees, this delicate balance is likely to be disrupted. In this case, some computer models show that the ice shelves along the ice sheet will lose increasing amounts of ice until not enough ice is available to maintain the shelves. At that point, the ice shelves would just keep losing ice, which could lead to the breakup of the West Antarctic Ice Sheet. That would have worldwide effects.

ANTARCTICA AND EARTH'S OCEANS

A massive meltdown of the West Antarctic Ice Sheet would affect the level of Earth's oceans. Scientists believe they know what sequence of events might lead to such a meltdown. First, it's important to understand that if all of Antarctica's ice *shelves* were to melt, they would *not* affect the sea level. That's because the ice contained in an ice shelf is already in the sea. It's like ice cubes in a glass of water. If, from the start, both cubes and water are already in the glass, as the ice cubes melt, the level of the liquid in the glass stays the same. However, if you *add* ice cubes to a glass already containing water, you will see that the level of the liquid rises and it stays at the higher level even after the ice has melted.

That scientific principle holds true for the Pine Island Ice *Shelf*. If it breaks up, the sea level will not rise. The problem arises when you add Pine Island Glacier, which flows on the mainland, to the equation. This rapidly moving glacier is carrying new ice toward the sea. Right now, the Pine Island Ice Shelf acts as a barrier. If the ice shelf were to collapse, it would no longer impede the glacier's flow. In this scenario, the glacier would flow directly into the sea—think of it as a refrigerator ice machine stuck in the On position.

An aerial photo shows icebergs on their seaward journey away from the Pine Island Ice Shelf.

An Antarctic seal poses with its newly fitted sensor. The sensor is attached with an adhesive that does not harm the animal.

Unexpected Scientists

Scientists using airplanes, boats, and AUVs continue to provide a wealth of information about the ocean that surrounds Antarctica. However, none of these vehicles can go long distances beneath the ice to collect information. That leaves a blind spot in our knowledge of the sea's deeper reaches. In the last few years, though, scientists have been collecting information about the Southern Ocean, sometimes called the Antarctic Ocean, with the help of some unusual scientific partners: Antarctic seals.

Some of these seals stay in the sea ice zone all winter. Their survival, of course, requires food. During an underwater hunt for food, seals can dive very deep into the ocean. Elephant seals are the best divers in Antarctica, diving up to 6,500 feet (2,000 m) deep. Not only do they dive deeply, but they can remain underwater for almost two hours. Truly amazing for a mammal!

Lars Boehme is a scientist who studies Antarctic ocean currents and also the behavior of seals. Surprisingly, diving seals can offer a lot of information about what's going on with ocean currents. "Employing seals to gather oceanographic data is, in some places, the only way to look into the ocean. And the best bit is that we learn a lot about these animals too!" Boehme explained. He and his seal collaborators gather this information with the use of small ocean sensors that are glued to the seal's head. (This does not harm the seal.)

For Boehme, catching the seals is a fun part of the project. "Elephant seals have no predator on land and are therefore very placid," said Boehme. The sensors are attached after the seals' annual molt, when they have shed their last year's coat. With slow, careful movements, Boehme creeps up on a snoozing seal, choosing an animal that is not near the water. When he is about 3 to 6 feet (1 to 2 m) from the seal, a quick puff of air through a blowpipe sends out a dart with a dose of anesthesia that sufficiently tranquilizes the seal so that the sensor can be attached within ten to fifteen minutes.

The sensing instrument is glued to the fur. "The glue we use never sets crystal hard and I always compare having a tag attached to the seal's fur with having chewing gum stuck in your hair. If you don't think about it, you do not know it is there. The seals could reach the sensor with their flippers, but they don't," Boehme stated. (And the following year, when the seal molts, the instrument falls off as the fur it's attached to falls out.) Boehme has observed some of the same animals year after year, and they do as well as the animals that have not been tagged.

The sensing instrument provides several different measurements. It records the water pressure surrounding the seal during each stage of a dive, from which Boehme can calculate the depth of the dive. Other sensors record the water temperature, the length of time each dive lasts, and if the seal is wet or dry.

"Seals do amazing things underwater, and with such a dive profile, we can look at how the dive is shaped, which could indicate if the seal was feeding, exploring, or travelling. The wet/dry sensors give us an idea if the seal is at sea or if it has hauled out onto an ice floe," said Boehme. This contributes to scientific knowledge about seal behaviors.

The combined data collected by the sensors also enables Boehme to determine information about the salinity and the density of the ocean water. "These are the main properties an oceanographer wants to know, as changes in density drive the ocean currents. The polar regions are very important for climate and the ocean currents. You can think of them as the pumps of the earth's heating system. Therefore, all scientists are very interested to get data from these places," Boehme added. Together, the unexpected partnership of seals and scientists is providing good "pictures" of how ocean currents are flowing beneath the ice and any changes they might be undergoing.

The many colored lines on this map of Antarctica show the travels of Antarctic seals fitted with sensors. The sensors not only tell scientists about seal behavior but also about ocean conditions.

British Antarctic Survey team members work on an AUV. The vehicle helps scientists collect data beneath the ice shelf near Pine Island Glacier.

That would cause the sea level to rise—just like ice cubes added to a glass of water. How much? If one-third of the West Antarctic Ice Sheet were added to the sea, climatologists think that it would raise sea levels world-wide by as much as 3 feet (0.9 m). That could inundate coastal cities and homes that are currently at sea level. If the entire West Antarctic Ice Sheet were to collapse, the rise in sea level would be much higher.

An increase in air temperature affects the melting rate of the ice. But scientists are also looking at another source—a hidden one—that may be contributing to the thinning of ice shelves. The Southern Ocean circulates around the whole of the continent. Evidence from instruments used to monitor water temperature suggests that the temperature of the Southern Ocean is rising. How might that affect the ice shelves? Scientists theorize that these slightly warmer currents flow beneath the ice shelves and are melting the ice from below. To gather evidence that will support or disprove this theory, scientists have inserted instruments into holes drilled into a thinning ice shelf like the one near Pine Island Glacier. The equipment remains in place after the scientists have left. The instruments monitor changes all year long, getting a complete record of annual changes, not just those that occur during the summer, when scientists can physically be present.

They are also monitoring ice shelves with other tools. In 2009 a group of scientists, led by Adrian Jenkins, a member of the British Antarctic Survey, explored the underside of the ice shelf near Pine Island Glacier with an AUV. Scientists hope the data collected during this exploration—such as water flow, temperature, and the level of salt in the water—plus the data collected by the instruments inserted through the drill holes will give them further insight into how and why the ice shelves are changing and, in some cases, collapsing.

Even as some scientists peek under the ice with AUVs, others have taken to the skies for a broader view of what's happening to Antarctic ice. Operation Ice Bridge is a project in which scientists from the National Aeronautics and Space Administration (NASA), the National Oceanic and Atmospheric Administration (NOAA), and a number of universities in the United States are working together to monitor the behavior of the Arctic and Antarctic ice. Operation Ice Bridge fills the time gap between an existing satellite program that has been measuring changes in polar ice, clouds, land elevation, and vegetation and a new satellite program scheduled to begin in 2014 to 2015.

In October and November 2009, a NASA DC-8 plane loaded with scientists and instruments such as ice-penetrating radar flew a series of missions over areas of Antarctica that appear to be undergoing rapid change. This included "mowing the grass"—flying in parallel lines—over the Pine Island Glacier and a series of crisscross flights over the Larsen C Ice Shelf. Now the project members are busy in their laboratories analyzing data about the thickness of the glaciers, ice shelves, and sea ice. From this information, scientists hope to gain a deeper understanding of how these different icy areas are responding to changes in Earth's climate system. Like the AUV used to peek under the ice shelf near Pine Island Glacier, this information could provide additional insight about the future of the West Antarctic Ice Sheet. Although scientists don't think the West Antarctic Ice Sheet is likely to collapse soon, the possibility that it might happen at all makes us realize that even though we may be far from Antarctica, changes there could affect the lives of many people.

The stability of Antarctica's ice also affects life-forms on Earth other than humans. The Southern Ocean encompasses all the ocean water south of 60° south latitude. You might think that such cold water couldn't contain much life, but these frigid waters are actually some of Earth's richest. The waters surrounding the ice shelves and icebergs are

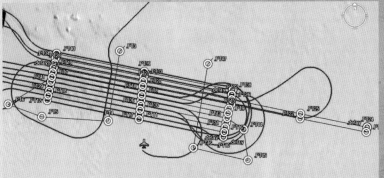

The surface of the Pine Island Glacier is fractured by thousands of crevasses *(top)*, making overland travel dangerous and almost impossible. To study changes in the glacier, researchers take measurements with lasers, radar, and other instruments from planes. This illustration *(above)* shows the flight plan (black lines) and the actual flight path (red lines) of a DC-8 aircraft as it made multiple measurement passes over the glacier. Researchers call this "mowing the grass."

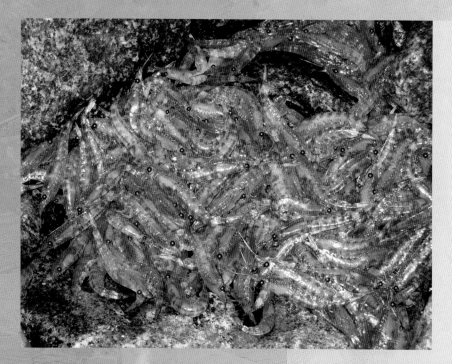

Krill are a crucial food source for most of the larger animals in the Southern Ocean. Fish, whales, seals, and penguins all depend on an abundant supply of krill, but changes in global climate threaten that supply.

fertile environments for small, shrimplike animals, called krill. Krill play an important part in the Antarctic food chain. Larger animals such as whales, seals, fish, and penguins depend on an abundant diet of krill for their survival. Without krill, these larger animals, many of which migrate to other areas and play important roles in distant ecosystems, will not survive. For their own survival, krill rely on sea ice. Krill eat the algae that grow on the bottom surface of sea ice, and the cracks and crevices in the ice provide hiding places that protect krill from predators. If the majority of sea ice were to melt, the krill population in the Southern Ocean could collapse. It's possible that in a domino effect, there would no longer be whales off the coast of California if the Southern Ocean krill population collapsed.

The Southern Ocean is more than just a home for animals, though. It is integral to the delicate balance of Antarctica's climate. An ocean current called the Antarctic Circumpolar Current (ACC) circulates around Antarctica from west to east, acting as a barrier between the continent and warmer ocean currents. The ACC helps keep Antarctica cold. The Antarctic Circumpolar Current is important for another reason. Very cold, deep currents flow out of the ACC and into the Atlantic, Pacific, and Indian oceans. Scientists have known about these currents for many years. In 2010 scientists from Australia and Japan reported startling new information about one of the deep cold water currents: how very powerful it is. The current they studied, which leaves the ACC and flows toward Australia, moves a volume of water that is equivalent to the flow of forty Amazon rivers. (At its mouth, the flow of the Amazon River, Earth's most powerful river, is about 8 trillion gallons, or 30 trillion liters, per day.) A flow this powerful can certainly affect other ocean currents.

This current and the other deep cold currents from Antarctica eventually make their way completely around the globe. If, in response to global warming, the temperature of the Antarctic Circumpolar Current rises, the flow pattern and direction of the ACC and its deep cold offshoots could change. This would likely cause Antarctica's climate and its marine-life habitats to change also. And because the deep cold currents are powerful and circulate globally, as they change, so might the flow patterns of currents in Earth's other oceans. In turn, those changes could affect everything from weather to the salinity of the water to the type of organisms that live in the waters and along the shorelines far from Antarctica.

WHY?

No doubt about it, Antarctica is a continent of extremes. Extreme cold. Extreme danger. Extreme isolation. But the continent's other extremes— extreme grandeur, extreme beauty, and extreme challenges—captivate people, luring them back, time after time. During her first trip to Antarctica, Robin Ellwood wrote in her journal "Antarctica is harsh, wild, tame, and gentle. It is bold and subtle, bleak and vibrant. Touch 'the ice' and one is forever changed and humbled."

Traveling many hours by plane, trekking across dangerous terrain, living in remote field camps, risking one's life in an under-ice dive, and drilling through seemingly endless depths of ice—clearly, research "on ice" is no picnic. So why do we do it? Why do scientists keep going back? Perhaps because Antarctica still has surprises, such as the Gamburtsev mountain range, in store. Although it was discovered during the International Geophysical Year in 1957–1958, it wasn't until the 2008–2009 field season that an international expedition was able to create the first detailed image of the range. For the first time, radar and other instruments show us the range's rugged peaks—the highest of which are still buried beneath 1,640 feet (500 m) of ice—and its deep valleys. How old is the Gamburtsev mountain range? How did it form? Both questions have scientists (with the help of twenty-four seismological stations located on the ice overlying the mountains) seeking the answers. What other surprises might the continent contain?

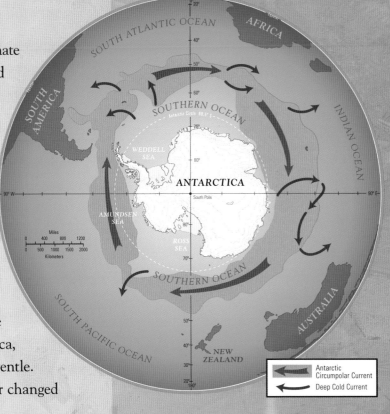

The powerful flow of the Antarctic Circumpolar Current helps keep the continent cold, but changes to it and the other deep cold currents that radiate from it affect oceans all over the globe.

Collecting data is a driving force for returning to Antarctica. "Natural systems are VERY complex. You can't study them in a couple of months and get all the data you need to understand completely how they work," explained Ross Powell. Antarctica is larger than Mexico and the forty-eight contiguous United States combined. Like the great variety of rock found throughout those areas, the same holds true for Antarctica. "To reconstruct past environments and climate history we need to travel to different places so we can get a more complete picture of what Antarctica was like. Different locations give us different 'windows' of time," he added.

Robin Ellwood returns because she loves learning and teaching. "I go back again and again to develop a better understanding of our world, to collaborate with a unique group of people who are trying to do so for us all. I want to model, for my middle school students and others, the importance of being a life-long learner—taking advantage of opportunities, taking reasonable risks, and getting involved—even when it requires extraordinary efforts."

It is important for everyone to remember that despite its location at the bottom of the world, Antarctica is not isolated from our lives. Its ocean currents, like fingers reaching outward, flow to all areas of Earth. For centuries, men and women have known of the dynamic forces at play on Antarctica, and we still strive to understand its mysteries. Water that flows beneath layers of ice. Tiny bubbles of unimaginably ancient air. Flowing ice streams that mimic earthquakes. Fossils that speak of ancient climates. And the tantalizing hope of undiscovered life-forms that may hold the keys to understanding how life survives in extreme ecosystems. Might any of these offer answers to crucial questions about our planet's future? Antarctica is a land of frozen secrets, with scarcely a handful completely divulged. The rest of those secrets, still locked inside the continent's icy cloak, offer us the promise of fascinating future discoveries.

Allan Ashworth examines a moss specimen under a microscope. His cold-weather gear dries on clotheslines hung from the ceiling of his Scott tent.

A British scientist stands in an ice cave at Faraday Station on Galindez Island.

WHEN I WAS IN COLLEGE, ONE OF MY GEOLOGY PROFESSORS VISITED ANTARCTICA. In those days, there were far fewer scientists on the continent than there are today. I remember talking with him about what a beautiful but almost other worldly place it was. His tales of the frozen land were magic. I was thrilled when he gave me a rock that he had collected there. Thirty-five years later, it remains an exotic treasure in my rock collection.

My Illinois home is far from Antarctica. However, in 1985 we got a taste of Antarctic-like weather. One morning, the temperature on the thermometer outside my back door was –27°F (–33°C). The windchill was close to –50°F (–46°C)! Nevertheless, with long hair still wet from my morning shower, I hauled our garbage cans out to the curb. In the twenty seconds it took to complete the chore, my hair froze solid. I was horrified. Yet extreme temperatures like this are routine for Antarctic researchers.

I have hiked in deep snow and camped in weather cold enough to freeze water, but I've never been to Antarctica. Fortunately, a number of my scientist friends have been there many times. I could not have written this book without their help. All of them graciously shared their work as well as their stories of life "on ice."

I would particularly like to thank ANDRILL investigators Dr. Ross Powell, Dr. Reed Scherer, and Dr. Matthew Olney for information on drilling in Antarctica. Louise Huffman, ANDRILL's education and outreach coordinator, answered questions about teacher participation.

Investigating Antarctic lakes would have been impossible without the help of Dr. Peter Doran and Dr. Martin J. Siegert. They patiently explained the special challenges of exploring water near the surface and deep below it. Thanks to Robin Ellwood, science teacher extraordinaire, for the many ways she brought the continent alive and to her student Maddie Cole for sharing her SCUBADooba Doo adventures.

The superlative specimens in the Fryxell Geology Museum at Augustana College, in Illinois, make it the absolutely best "waiting room" in the world. Thanks to collections curator Susan Kornreich-Wolf and Dr. William Hammer for answering a thousand questions about dinosaur hunting. Dr. Hammer's paleontology lab is fascinating. It, however, is completely dwarfed by the fully assembled *Cryolophosaurus* skeleton nearby. Sharp teeth and talons are a truly impressive way to greet visitors.

Thanks to Dr. Douglas Wiens for explaining the dynamics of the Whillans Ice Stream. His new adventures, mapping and investigating the Gamburtsev Mountains, are sure to be equally eye-opening. Thanks, also, to Dr. Allan Ashworth, for supplying the crucial details of his work in the Dry Valleys. I'd have been "lost at sea" without Dr. Stephen Rintoul's help on the Antarctic Circumpolar Current and its deep, cold current offshoots. Last, but not least, thanks to Dr. Lars Boehme for sharing seal stories and his photo of the seal—perhaps a glimpse of Antarctica's playful side.

In 2009 I was invited to attend the Antarctic Treaty Summit, in Washington, D.C. There, we celebrated the fiftieth anniversary of the signing of the Antarctic Treaty. We drafted, approved, and signed the Forever Declaration, a document that reiterates the view "that Antarctica should remain a continent devoted to international co-operation, the pursuit of scientific endeavor, and that it should be used exclusively for peaceful purposes." I listened to scientists recap highlights of Antarctic investigation. I heard lawmakers discuss future politics and how they might affect the continent. The scientists and lawmakers were not always in agreement. Yet despite their differences, they all agreed in one area: it is crucial that people everywhere should be informed about what has been learned about Antarctica. Information must be shared in ways that people can understand, so they will care about Antarctica and its future. I hope that *Frozen Secrets* may be a step toward achieving that goal.

A member of Robert Falcon Scott's Terra Nova Expedition drives a dog sled past a huge ice formation on Ross Island.

autonomous underwater vehicle (AUV): a robot that travels underwater

bedrock: solid rock that is beneath loose material such as soil

calving: the separation of a piece of ice from a larger ice mass

carbon dioxide: a chemical compound containing two atoms of oxygen bonded to each atom of carbon. Carbon dioxide is a gas present in the atmosphere. This gas is produced by the burning of fuels and used in photosynthesis by plants.

cirque: bowl-shaped basins carved in rock by ice

climate: the pattern of weather conditions typical of a particular area

climatologist: a scientist who studies climate

core sample: a long, narrow column of material obtained by drilling deeply with a hollow tube. In Antarctica the drill gathers samples from many different layers of ice that formed millions of years ago.

crevasse: a deep crack or chasm

diatoms: microscopic algae that live in freshwater or salt water

firn: snow that has lost half of its air spaces and lasted at least one summer without completely melting and refreezing as ice

frostbite: a very painful injury that results from exposing the body—especially the ears, the nose, the hands, and the feet—to extreme cold

geologist: a person who studies rocks

glacial ice: ice that contains less than 20 percent air

glacier: a mass of ice that moves slowly through mountain valleys or over land

glaciologist: a person who studies glacial ice

global positioning system (GPS): a system of satellites and receivers that determines location

global warming: a worldwide increase in Earth's average temperature

Gondwanaland: a pre-historic continent that contained modern-day Antarctica

ice ages: periods when Earth experiences extremely cold weather and when much of its surface is covered by snow and ice

iceberg: a piece of ice that floats in the sea. In some cases, only a small part of the iceberg can be seen above the ocean's surface.

ice-penetrating radar: a tool that measures ice depth

ice sheet: a vast, flat mass of ice and snow that covers a large land area

ice shelf: a large, thick piece of floating ice that is attached to a coastline

ice streams: channels of ice that form within larger ice masses. These channels flow faster than the surrounding ice.

interglacial period: a time of warmer temperatures between ice ages

katabatic wind: a fierce wind caused by the rapid flow of cold air down a mountain slope

krill: shrimplike animals that are the main source of food for whales

laser altimeter: an instrument that measures small changes in elevation

latitude: the distance between imaginary lines north and south of the equator. Latitude is used to determine location.

lichen: a complex, colorful plant made up of an alga and a fungus growing together on a solid surface

meltwater: water that melts from a large mass of ice

methane: a greenhouse gas produced by natural processes and human activities

moss: small soft plants that typically grow close together

paleobotanist: a scientist who studies ancient plant life

paleontologist: a scientist who studies prehistoric life

Pangaea: a supercontinent that existed 350 to 200 million years ago

particulates: soot, ash, and other solid particles that are a component of air pollution

precipitation: water—including rain, snow, sleet, and hail—that falls to Earth from the atmosphere

retreat: relating to glaciers; to melt and consequently cover a smaller land area

scuba: a type of diving where divers use a self-contained underwater breathing apparatus

sea ice: ice that forms on the ocean when surface waters freeze

sea level: a measure of ocean water volume. Sea level measurements show how high onto land the ocean reaches.

sediments: particles of soil and small pieces of broken rock. If they are suspended in water, they eventually sink to form a solid layer on the bottom of an ocean, a lake, or a river.

seismograph: a tool that records seismic waves, typically the energy waves of an earthquake

silica: a naturally made chemical compound that contains silicon and oxygen

sonde: a piece of equipment that contains sensitive scientific instruments

topography: surface features, such as hills and rivers, that are found in an area

ventifact: a rock sculpted by wind

SOURCE NOTES

7   Robert Falcon Scott, *Scott's Last Expedition: The Journals* (New York: Carroll & Graf Publishers, 1996), 395.

8   Ibid., 430.

8   Ibid., 440.

11   William Hammer, interview by author, December 5, 2005.

16   Robin Ellwood, e-mail to author, September 6, 2008.

17   Peter Athans, e-mail to author, February 15, 2010.

17   Ross Powell, interview by author, July 6, 2009.

17–18   Ibid.

18   Ibid.

20   Roald Amundsen. *The South Pole: An Account of the Norwegian Antarctic Expedition in the Fram, 1910–1912* (Breman: Salzwasser-Verlag im Europäischen Hochschulverlag, 2010), 222.

20   Robin Ellwood, e-mail to author, January 31, 2010.

21   William Hammer, e-mail to author, February 4, 2010.

36   Douglas Wiens, e-mail to author, September 21, 2008.

36   Douglas Wiens, e-mail to author, December 10, 2009.

36   Wiens, e-mail to author, September 21, 2008.

37   Ibid.

37   Ibid.

44   Powell, interview by author, July 6, 2009.

44   Ross Powell, interview by author, September 22, 2008.

45   Ibid.

46   Ibid.

49   Peter Doran, e-mail to author, August 12, 2009.

50   Peter Doran, e-mail to author, September 2, 2008.

50   Robin Ellwood, e-mail to author June 22, 2009.

51   Ellwood, e-mail to author, September 6, 2008.

51   Doran, e-mail to author, September 2, 2008,

51   Ellwood, e-mail to author, September 6, 2008.

51   Doran, e-mail to author, September 2, 2008.

51–52   Ellwood, e-mail to author, September 6, 2008.

52   Ellwood, e-mail to author, January 31, 2010.

52   Doran, e-mail to author, September 2, 2008.

52   Ellwood, e-mail to author, June 22, 2009.

53   Doran, e-mail to author, September 2, 2008.

54–55   Robin Ellwood, blog on Polar Trek: Teachers and Researchers Exploring and Collaborating, November 21, 2008, http://www.polartrec.com/, Ellwood's blog, http://www.polartrec.com/node/7148 (June 30, 2009).

60   Maddie Cole, e-mail to author, July 27, 2009.

60–61   Ibid.

61   Robin Ellwood, e-mail to author, July 7, 2009.

61   Cole, e-mail to author, July 27, 2009.

67   Martin Siegert, e-mail to author on note on September 2, 2008.

68   Ibid.

74   William Hammer, e-mail to author, May 15, 2009.

75   William Hammer, e-mail to author, May 18, 2009.

75   Hammer, interview by author December 5, 2005.

75   Ibid.

81   Allan Ashworth, e-mail to author, July 7, 2009.

81   Ibid.

83   Ibid.

84   Scott, *Scott's Last Expedition*, 243–244.

90–91   Lars Boehme, e-mail to author, January 29, 2010.

91   Ibid.

91   Ibid.

91   Ibid.

91   Ibid.

95   Ellwood, e-mail to author, January 31, 2010.

96   Ross Powell, e-mail to author, January 31, 2010.

96   Ellwood, e-mail to author, January 31, 2010.

SELECTED BIBLIOGRAPHY

ARTICLES

Amos, Jonathan. "Deep Ice Tells Long Ago Climate Story." BBC News. September 4, 2006. http://news.bbc.co.uk/2/hi/science/nature/5314592.stm (September 15, 2008).

Augustin, L., S. Panichi, and F. Frascati. "EPICA Dome C 2 Drilling Operations: Performances, Difficulties, Results." Annals of Glaciology 47, no. 1 (December 2007): 68–72. http://www.igsoc.org/annals/47/a47a005.pdf (July 6, 2009).

Bindschadler, Robert A., and Charles R. Bentley. "On Thin Ice." Scientific American 287, no. 6 (December 2002): 98–105.

Corr, Hugh F. J., and David G. Vaughan. "A Recent Volcanic Eruption beneath the West Antarctic Ice Sheet." Nature Geoscience 1, no. 2 (February 2008): 122–125.

Cúneo, N. R., E. L. Taylor, T. N. Taylor, and M. Krings. "An In Situ Fossil Forest from the Upper Fremouw Formation (Triassic) of Antarctica: Paleoenvironmental Setting and Paleoclimate Analysis." Palaeogeography, Palaeoclimatology, Palaeoecology 197, no. 3–4 (2003): 239–261.

Dieter Lüthi, Martine Le Floch, Bernhard Bereiter, Thomas Blunier, Jean-Marc Barnola, Urs Siegenthaler, Dominique Raynaud, et al. "High-Resolution Carbon Dioxide Concentration Record 650,000–800,000 Years before Present." Nature 453 (May 15, 2008): 379–382.

European Project for Ice Coring in Antarctica (EPICA). "Eight Glacial Cycles from an Antarctic Ice Core." Nature 429 (June 10, 2004): 623–628.

Fox, Douglas. "Freeze-Dried Findings Support a Tale of Two Ancient Climates." Science 320 (May 30, 2008): 1,152–1,154.

Fukamachi, Y., S. R. Rintoul, J. A. Church, S. Aoki, S. Sokolov, M. A. Rosenberg, and M. Wakatsuchi. "Strong Export of Antarctic Bottom Water East of the Kerguelen Plateau." Nature Geoscience 3, no. 5 (2010): 327–331.

Gosnell, Mariana. "The Last Unexplored Place on Earth." Discover Magazine, November 2007.

Hammer, W. R. "New Therapsids from the Upper Fremouw Formation of Antarctica." Journal of Vertebrate Paleontology 15, no. 1 (March 1995): 105–112.

———. "Triassic Terrestrial Vertebrate Faunas of Antarctica," in T. N. Taylor and E. L. Taylor, eds. Antarctica Paleobiology: Its Role in the Reconstruction of Gondwanaland. New York: Springer-Verlag, 1990.

———. "Jurassic Dinosaurs from Antarctica: Another Puzzling High Latitude Fauna." Abstract. Vol. 193. Geological Society of America, 1992 annual meeting, Cincinnati, OH. Boulder, CO.

Hammer, W. R., J. W. Collinson, and William J. Ryan. "A New Triassic Vertebrate Fauna from Antarctica and Its Depositional Setting." Antarctica Science 2, no. 2 (June 1990): 163–169.

Hammer, W. R., and W. J. Hickerson. "Comments on the Fossil Vertebrates from the Falla Formation (Jurassic), Beardmore Glacier Region, Antarctica." Antarctic Journal of the U.S. 27, no. 5 (1992): 1.

———. "A Crested Theropod Dinosaur from Antarctica." Science 264, no. 5160 (May 6, 1994): 828–830.

McManus, H. A., E. L. Taylor, T. N. Taylor, and J. W. Collinson. "A Petrified Glossopteris Flora from Collinson Ridge, Central Transantarctic Mountains: Late Permian or Early Triassic?" Review of Palaeobotany and Palynology 120, no. 3–4 (July 30, 2002): 233–246.

Mikucki, Jill A., and John C. Priscu. "Bacterial Diversity Associated with Blood Falls, a Subglacial Outflow from the Taylor Glacier, Antarctica." Applied and Environmental Microbiology 73, no. 12 (June 2007): 4,029–4,039. Available online at http://www.pubmedcentral.nih.gov/articlerender.fcgi?artid=1932727 (July 1, 2009).

Siegert, Martin J. "Sunless Seas." Geoscientist Online. October 2007. http://www.geolsoc.org.uk/index.html (August 10, 2008).

Vogel, Stefan W. "Fire and Ice." Nature Geoscience 1, no.2 (February 2008): 91–92.

BOOKS

Alley, Richard B. The Two-Mile Time Machine: Ice Cores, Abrupt Climate Change, and Our Future. Princeton, NJ: Princeton University Press, 2000.

Alley, Richard B., and Robert A. Bindschadler, eds. The West Antarctic Ice Sheet: Behavior and Environment. Antarctic Research Series. Vol. 77. Washington, DC: American Geophysical Union, 2001.

Bargagli, Roberto. Antarctic Ecosystems. Berlin: Springer-Verlag, 2005.

Belanger, Dian Olson. Deep Freeze: The United States, the International Geophysical Year, and the Origins of Antarctica's Age of Science. Boulder: University Press of Colorado, 2006.

Campbell, David G. The Crystal Desert. Boston: Houghton Mifflin Co., 1992.

Fogg, G. E. A History of Antarctic Science. Cambridge, UK: University Press, 1992.

Griffiths, Tom. Slicing the Silence: Voyaging to Antarctica. Cambridge, MA: Harvard University Press, 2007.

King, Lester C. *Wandering Continents and Spreading Sea Floors on an Expanding Earth.* New York: John Wiley and Sons, 1983.

Nield, Ted. *Supercontinent: Ten Billion Years in the Life of Our Planet.* Cambridge, MA: Harvard University Press, 2007.

Scott, Robert Falcon. *Scott's Last Expedition: The Journals.* New York: Carroll & Graf Publishers, 1996.

Zotikov, Igor A. *The Antarctic Subglacial Lake Vostok: Glaciology, Biology, and Planetology.* Berlin: Springer Praxis Publishing, 2006.

FURTHER READING AND WEBSITES
BOOKS

Armstrong, Jennifer. *Shipwreck at the Bottom of the World.* New York: Crown Books, 2000.

Cherry, Lynne, and Gary Braasch. *How We Know What We Know about Our Changing Climate: Scientists and Kids Explore Global Warming.* Nevada City, CA: Dawn Publications, 2008.

Conlan, Kathy. *Under the Ice: A Marine Biologist at Work.* Toronto, ON: Kids Can Press, 2002.

Flannery, Tim, and Sally M. Walker. *We Are the Weather Makers: The History of Climate Change.* Cambridge, MA: Candlewick Press, 2009.

Gore, Al. *An Inconvenient Truth: The Crisis of Global Warming.* New York: Viking, 2007.

Johnson, Rebecca L. *Ernest Shackleton: Gripped by the Antarctic.* Minneapolis: Twenty-First Century Books, 2003.

Johnson, Rebecca L. *Investigating Climate Change: Scientists' Search for Answers in a Warming World.* Minneapolis: Twenty-First Century Books, 2009.

Latta, Sara L. *Ice Scientist: Careers in the Frozen Antarctic.* Berkeley Heights, NJ: Enslow, 2009.

Silverstein, Alvin, Virginia Silverstein, and Laura Silverstein Nunn. *Global Warming.* Minneapolis: Twenty-First Century Books, 2009.

Time. *Global Warming.* Minneapolis: Twenty-First Century Books, 2008.

Webb, Sophie. *My Season with Penguins.* Boston: Houghton Mifflin, 2000.

WEBSITES

Antarctic Geological Drilling (ANDRILL)
http://www.andrill.org/education
This website has an excellent section for educators and students.

British Antarctic Survey
http://www.antarctica.ac.uk/
Read about what daily life is like for researchers in Antarctica as well as information about wildlife and geography.

ENDURANCE
http://www.evl.uic.edu/endurance/endurance.html
Through this website, you can read Vickie Siegel's blog of the ENDURANCE mission.

National Aeronautics and Space Administration/ National Science Foundation
http://pigiceshelf.nasa.gov/, http://www.espo.nasa.gov/oib/
These sites have information about Pine Island Glacier and Operation Ice Bridge, respectively. Also, NASA has an excellent series of short videos of the flyovers done by the scientists participating in the project, available at http://www.youtube.com/user/NASAtelevision#g/c/51B68159A46E7859.

National Ice Core Laboratory, University of New Hampshire
http://www.nicl-smo.unh.edu/index.html
Learn how ice cores are stored as well as the process a scientist must use to get an ice core for experimentation.

National Science Foundation: Animation of East Antarctic Ice Sheet Growth
http://www.nsf.gov/news/news_videos.jsp?cntn_id=114172&media_id=64634
Visit this website to watch video animation of what may cause ice sheets to grow.

Polar Trek: Teachers and Researchers, Exploring and Collaborating
http://www.polartrec.com/lake-ecosystems-in-antarctica/journals/robin-ellwood
Robin Ellwood's Journal blog is available at this site.

United States Antarctic Program: The Antarctic Sun
http://antarcticsun.usap.gov/
Explore articles dealing with a variety of issues concerning Antarctica, ranging from wildlife to funding projects.

United States Geological Survey: Landsat Image Mosaic of Antarctica (LIMA)
http://lima.usgs.gov/
Visit Antarctica virtually through wonderful, high resolution satellite images of all areas of the continent.

United States Ice Drilling Program
http://www.icedrill.org/
Find out more about the process of obtaining ice samples and ice cores. The site offers a list of equipment used and a list of current drilling and sampling projects.

Amundsen, Roald, 7, 20
ANDRILL project, 44–46
animal life, 72, 73–78, 82, 94
Antarctic Circumpolar Current (ACC), 94–95
Antarctic Treaty (1961), 14–16
Ashworth, Allan, 79–81, 83, 96
Athans, Peter, 17
autonomous underwater vehicles (AUVs), 53–59, 92–93

bathrooms, proper location of, 21
BEDMAP project, 43
bedrock, 43–46
Boehme, Lars, 90–91
Bot House, 54–55

carbon dioxide, 85–86
climate patterns, 32, 44, 84; ocean currents and, 94–95; prehistoric Antarctica and, 70–71, 78, 81–82, 83; warming trends and, 85–89
clothing, 17–19, 49–50
Cole, Maddie, 60–61
Cook, James, 12–13
Cryolophosaurus ellioti (dinosaur), 76–78

Davis, John, 13
diatom fossils, 81–82
dinosaurs, 73–78
Doran, Peter, 23, 48–49, 50–52, 53, 56, 58, 62, 84
drilling projects, 30–33
Dry Valleys, 46–49

East Antarctic Ice Sheet, 28, 40
Elliot, David, 74, 76
Ellwood, Robin, 16, 20, 23, 50–52, 54–55, 95, 96
ENDURANCE (AUV), 53–59

European Project for Ice Coring in Antarctica (EPICA), 30, 31–32
exploration of Antarctica, 6–8, 12–13, 14

fire, dangers of, 17
food and supplies, 8, 11, 14
fossils, prehistoric Antarctica and, 70–82
frostbite, dangers of, 17–18
Fuchs, Vivian, 14

Gamburtsev mountain range, 95
geothermal heat, 33, 64
glaciers, 26–27, 28, 87–88, 89, 92, 93
Glossopteris plants, 71–72
greenhouse gases, climate patterns and, 85–86

Hammer, William, 11, 21, 73–78
Happy Camper School, 19–21

ice: creation of, 25–27; floating ice, 39–41; ice cores and, 30–33; measuring thickness of, 29; movement of, 33–38; South Pole and, 24–25; spread of, 28, 46
icebergs, 40–41
ice cores, 30–33, 85–86
ice domes, 30, 31–33
ice sheets: East Antarctic Ice Sheet, 28, 40; subglacial lakes and, 62–69; West Antarctic Ice Sheet, 30, 34, 40–41, 45
ice shelves, 34, 38, 39–41, 87–89, 92
ice streams, 34
International Geophysical Year (IGY), 14

Jenkins, Adrian, 92

krill, 94

Lake Bonney, 48, 49, 52, 53–59, 62
Lake Ellsworth, 66–69

lakes, 47–55, 62–69, 79–80
Lake Vostok, 63–66
land formations: bedrock, 43–46; Dry Valleys, 46–49; glacial ice and, 27, 28; mapping, 42–43; robot exploration and, 56–59, 60–61
laser altimeters, 63
Lewis, Adam, 79, 83
life-forms: Dry Valleys and, 47; microorganisms, 65–66, 68–69, 81–82, 94; prehistoric Antarctica, 70–82; Southern Ocean and, 93–95; subglacial lakes and, 65–66, 68–69; surface lakes and, 52
Lystrosaurus (extinct animal), 72–73

maps, 10, 12, 13, 38, 43, 70, 84, 91, 95
Marchant, David, 79
methane gas, 85–86
microorganisms, 65–66, 68–69, 81–82, 94
mountain climbing, 17

Nothofagus trees, 80–81

Oates, Lawrence, 8
ocean currents, 92, 94–95
Operation Ice Bridge, 93
ostracod fossils, 82

Pangaea, 70
Pine Island Glacier, 87–88, 89, 92, 93
plant life, 71–72, 79–82
pollen fossils, 80–81
Powell, Ross, 17–18, 44–46, 96
prehistoric Antarctica, 70–83

radar, 29, 42–43
robotic explorations, 53–59, 60–61, 92–93
rock cores, 44–46
Ross Ice Shelf, 34, 40–41

Scherer, Reed, 21, 86
Scott, Robert Falcon, 6–8, 71, 84
scuba diving, 49–52
SCUBADooba Doo device, 60–61
sea ice, 39–41
sea levels, 24, 89, 92
seals, 51, 90–91
search and rescue techniques, 19–20
sediment drilling, 18, 44, 45
seismographs, 34–37, 42–43
Shackleton, Ernest, 21, 53, 86
shelters, 17, 19, 21, 22, 75
Siegert, Martin, 67–69
snow, 25–26
Southern Ocean, 92, 93–95
South Pole, 7, 24–25
stick-slip motion, ice streams and, 35–37
stratigraphy, 45, 82
subglacial lakes, 62–69
surface lakes, 47–55, 62, 79–80
survival training, 19–21

Taylor, Edith, 71–72
temperatures, 6, 48, 56–57, 92
thickness, of ice, 28, 29, 30, 40, 43, 64
tourism, 11–12, 16

Vinson Massif, 17
volcanic eruptions, 78, 82–83

warming trends, 85–89
weather, 6, 11, 12, 16, 74, 75. See also climate patterns
West Antarctic Ice Sheet, 30, 34, 40–41, 45, 87, 88–89, 92
Whillans Ice Stream, 35–37
Wiens, Douglas, 17, 35–37